DEFENDING DONALD HARVEY

The Case of America's
Most Notorious
Angel-of-Death
Serial Killer

William Whalen, attorney, and Bruce Martin

DEFENDING
DONALD HARVEY

emmis
books

Emmis Books
1700 Madison Road
Cincinnati, Ohio 45206

www.emmisbooks.com

Library of Congress Cataloging-in-Publication Data

Whalen, William, 1941–
Defending Donald Harvey : the case of America's most notorious
angel-of-death serial killer / William Whalen and Bruce Martin ;
foreword by Pat Minarcin.
    p. cm.
Includes index.
ISBN 1-57860-209-2 (pbk.)
1. Harvey, Donald, 1952- 2. Serial murderers–Ohio–Case studies.
3. Serial murderers–Kentucky–Case studies. I. Martin, Bruce, 1922–
II. Title.
HV6533.05W43 2005
364.152'3'092–dc22

2005001725

Cover photo and trial photos courtesy of the *Cincinnati Enquirer*

Photo of The Warren County [Ohio] Correctional Facility courtesy of The Warren County [Ohio] Correctional Facility

Editor: Jack Heffron
Photo Editor: Connie Springer
Cover and Book Designer: Kelly N. Kofron

ACKNOWLEDGMENTS

The authors thank Judy Pettigrew and Mary Lou Ackerman for bringing us together for this project. We thank our agent, Emilie Jacobson, Senior Vice President, Curtis Brown, Ltd., for her helpful guidance, especially her advice on voice. We thank our editor, Jack Heffron, for valuable suggestions on improving our manuscript, especially his insight about not letting the events obscure the people.

We owe a special debt to Graydon DeCamp, who conducted extensive interviews and graciously turned over to us, with his blessing, the fruits of his research.

We thank Pat Minarcin for his role in this story and for writing the Afterword.

More people than we can name contributed to this work through the information they provided in interviews. We want to mention especially Dr. Lee Lehman, Lt. Bill Fletcher, and Marie Eveleigh.

The staff members at Warren Correctional Institution, Richard Jesko in particular, have been especially helpful to us in providing access to Donald Harvey in the penitentiary for confidential interviews.

We thank Paula Ehemann for her help with arrangements and communications.

Completion of this project would not have been possible without the encouragement, editorial assistance, and proofreading of Phyllis Martin.

And, finally, we thank Donald Harvey for his cooperation through providing information by interviews and in writing and by reviewing our manuscript for errors. He wanted this book to be written, although he knew he could receive no material benefit from its publication.

CONTENTS

This story is true—incredible, but true.

We have taken some artistic license in recreating scenes and dialogue, but we have changed no material facts. We have changed a few names for legal reasons or to spare living persons additional pain. The first time we used any fictitious name, we indicated the substitution with an asterisk.

PROLOGUE
by William Whalen

I didn't choose to be the defense attorney for a serial killer. Neither did Judge Ralph Winkler intend to place me in that position when he appointed me public defender for nursing assistant Donald Harvey, who had confessed to killing a terminally ill patient in a county hospital.

We expected a routine case, of little interest to anyone other than the principals, except for the public suggestion that the death might be considered a mercy killing. Both of us were shocked when the sapling he assigned me to tend turned out to have the roots of a giant sequoia. That death was the third-to-last in a series of more than fifty deaths Harvey caused during an eighteen-year murderous career in three hospitals in two states.

Our system of criminal justice requires that a defendant in a felony case have legal representation. The process is adversarial—prosecution versus defense—and a defendant without an attorney would be at a serious disadvantage. If the defendant does not have an attorney, the judge will appoint one to balance the scales of justice.

As a defense attorney, I am by definition on the side of the accused. My duty is to obtain the best possible outcome for the defendant. Decisions about guilt or innocence are the province of the judge and the jury. Not the attorneys.

Because I was a prosecutor before I became a defense attorney, I am thoroughly familiar with the court system. I understand the motivations of the prosecutor and the flexibility in the process. In other words, I know how to use that flexibility to obtain the best outcomes for my clients. I do whatever it takes within the law to free my clients or minimize their punishment. To do less would be a violation of the ethics of my profession. People who have made up their minds that a defendant is guilty may think I am a roadblock to justice. But they wouldn't want to be without a defense attorney's services if they were the accused, guilty or not.

I accept public disapproval as part of the job. I do not seek public attention. I am not a flamboyant courtroom performer. I do not indulge in histrionics in front of a jury. Nor do I offer catchy slogans in rhyme.

People who get their legal education from television do not realize that many cases never come to trial. The attorneys negotiate settlements through plea bargaining.

This procedure avoids the uncertainties of a jury trial. The prosecution accepts a sure conviction on a lesser charge rather than take the risk of an acquittal. The defense accepts a negotiated penalty in order to escape the possibility of an even harsher penalty. The public is also served, because the punishment is certain. Furthermore, the taxpayers save money by avoiding the courtroom and jury expenses of a lengthy trial. The savings are especially evident when taxpayers are paying the attorneys on both sides. Court-appointed public defenders are paid by the county, with a partial reimbursement by the state. Plea bargaining is a key part of my arsenal.

Donald Harvey's case seemed simple. The police had developed strong evidence and obtained a confession. I prepared to challenge the confession but thought there was little chance of success. I had nothing to offer in a plea bargain. I decided to base our strategy on the mercy killing aspect, hoping for a sympathetic jury that would acquit him or recommend a lighter sentence because of that mitigating circumstance.

As you will learn when you read this book, Pat Minarcin, TV news anchor, raised a question on the air: Had Donald Harvey killed more than one?

In retrospect, the question was obvious. Experience shows that a medical attendant who kills a patient almost never stops at one death. I asked Harvey that question and was horrified at his answer. The number was so large that he could only estimate how many he had killed.

The strategy I had planned was no longer tenable. The probability that other murders would be discovered posed an unacceptable risk for Harvey. The possibility that a serial killer might go free to commit more murders would present a public relations nightmare for the Hamilton County prosecutor, an elected official.

The police knew of no suspicious deaths to investigate. Harvey's knowledge of the identities of the victims provided leverage for a plea bargain. With Harvey's concurrence, I set a goal of avoiding the death penalty.

Donald Harvey's life became irrevocably entwined with mine. Years after the events reported here, we are still regularly in contact. He trusts me and considers me a friend, the father he never had. I don't understand him, but I care for his welfare and still act to protect him. Donald wants his story told.

Bruce Martin and I have been as objective as possible in presenting this story. The bulk of the account is reporting, based on hours of videotapes and audiotapes, official documents, correspondence, and interviews. Whenever I am personally engaged in the action, we have switched to a first-person narration to signal my involvement.

PART I

MURDER ONE

1. Direction from the Otherworld

Donald Harvey needed privacy for his ceremony. He rechecked to be certain that he had locked and bolted the door to his trailer. He locked the door to his bedroom for extra security. He was careful to exclude light and any stray air current that might produce a false signal. After pulling the heavy draperies across the closed windows, he tugged at the edges to eliminate any gaps. Although the room was cramped, his habitual neatness always resulted in an appearance of order.

Satisfied with these precautions, Donald stripped and dressed in his long black robe, adjusting the fit and smoothing the wrinkles. He needed to look right in order to feel right. He was handsome, with his dark curly hair and slim, erect posture. His pale face contrasted with his ebony robe. Although there was no one to see, in the dim light his enlarged pupils had an inky depth of mystery.

He cleared all articles from the top of his dressing table and spread two black cloths completely covering the surface. He knew that attention to details of proper procedure was critical for eliminating negative forces whenever he conducted a ceremony.

He set the skull on an antique plate in the middle of the table. He liked the skull, even though it was missing several teeth and the top had been cut off during the autopsy from which it had been saved. The skull was anonymous, and Donald didn't assign it any identity. It was just a skull, although it had once housed the brains of a living human being.

Presumably the pathologist at the Veterans Administration hospital who put the skull in his collection once knew its origin, but any identification had long been lost. Donald had acquired the skull during a housecleaning of the hospital morgue. His supervisor didn't know he had appropriated one skull for his own use when given a batch to take to the crematorium.

Donald placed a black candle in the skull and arranged four black candles in candlesticks. In front of the skull he put a brass incense burner, a perforated globe on a pedestal. It rested on a clear glass ashtray never sullied by tobacco ashes.

He set out two crystal goblets, one for wine and one for water. The goblets were special, never used for any other purpose. Beside the wine goblet he placed the Waterford crystal decanter of red wine he always kept in the back of his cabinet.

Next he put his Egyptian ankh (i.e., a cross with a loop on top, symbolizing life) on the altar behind the skull. He was especially proud of the ankh he had made many years ago from weeping willows cut and woven in the springtime, when the sap was up. He laid two knives on the altar. One had a white handle; the other, black. The black-handled knife was special to him. He had made it himself and had etched symbols on the blade with hydrochloric acid—his moon sign and birth sign, and his name in runic characters. He never actually used the knives in his ceremonies, because he didn't practice any sacrifices. Neither did he use any human parts as some others did.

To complete the preparation of his altar, Donald took out his *Book of Shadows*, black, with an embossed gold pentagram. *The Book of Shadows* was his personal record book in which he entered in his own handwriting all his ceremonies, his favorite prayers, short poems, and quotations he favored.

Donald added one other precaution, his own innovation not found in any of his books nor used in any ceremonies he'd witnessed. He donned a surgical mask covering his mouth and nose. He wanted to avoid any disturbance of the air in the room that might be caused by his own breathing.

He lit the candles and the incense and turned out all the other lights in the room. The candles cast flickering shadows as he moved.

He always began his ceremony by drawing his circles, starting with the inner circle around him. Sometimes he drew the circles with salt, sulfur, or sand. His choice was based on the type of ceremony, because different spirits had different aversions.

At other times, he'd use no physical markings, just shut his eyes and draw the circles in his mind. He liked to follow the prescribed rituals as closely as possible, but he had to make concessions to practicality. He obviously could not draw in his trailer the nine-foot circle of the ancient tradition. Tonight he chose to imagine the circle as a yellow cone surrounding him.

He followed the steps of his ritual and summoned Duncan, his protective spirit from the other world. He had met Duncan when he attended a training program dedicated to the practice of satanic worship at New Bern, North Carolina, and was initiated into the secret society. Donald always felt himself to be in complete control of the ceremony. He once told a friend, "Duncan has never controlled me. I control him. Spirits can control you if you let them. Sometimes I'd spend an hour on the ceremony and then break it because it didn't feel right."

He felt Duncan's presence, but he asked for a sign. The candle in the skull flickered.

Donald addressed the skull, "I did Joseph Pike last night with adhesive cleaner. He died a few hours later, before the end of my shift." There was no response. Duncan didn't always respond when Donald reported, even when he had chosen the victim.

Donald took out his handwritten list of four names, all of them patients in his care at Daniel Drake Memorial Hospital. "Okay, here are the critically ill patients. Show me by some sign, a flicker of the candle or something. For the first candle, Hilda Leitz." No response. "Okay, second candle. Pamela Anishinsel." No response. "Third candle, John Powell." The candle on the right of the skull flickered. "Fourth candle, Raphael Giron." He thought the last candle flickered slightly.

"Which one do you want?"

The third candle flickered again.

Donald had his direction. Powell. He ended the ceremony. He extinguished the candles and the incense and put away all his paraphernalia. He removed his robe and hung it in his closet. After dressing, he opened a window for a few minutes to disperse the scent from the incense and the candles.

But the flickering candle remained in his mind.

2. An Expected Death

The next morning, Saturday, March 7, 1987, Donald took a bottle of cyanide crystals from its hiding place in his trailer. He filled a small vial. Working under his oven hood to avoid inhaling any fumes, he added water to dissolve the crystals and watched the solution turn amber. He put the vial in his pocket.

That Saturday Harvey was scheduled to work the first shift, 7:00 A.M. to 3:00 P.M., in the Skilled Nursing Facility at Drake. Upon his arrival at the hospital, he went first to the locker room and put his lunch in his locker. Because he was early—he usually was—no one else was in the locker room.

He checked his appearance and combed his hair. Appearance was important. Not to the patients—most of them were unaware of what went on around them. And Harvey didn't care what the staff thought so long as he didn't attract any unwanted attention to himself. No, his appearance was important to him for his own sake. Harvey was always neat about his person. He liked the way he looked in his crisp white nurse's uniform.

He walked through the ward, stopping to look in on John Powell in ward C-300. He felt sorry for Powell, lying there sprouting life-support tubes. Powell had a gastrostomy feeding tube, a tracheotomy tube for breathing, an IV for medication, and a urinary catheter. He even had a Blanketrol, a special cooling blanket.

John Powell was strikingly different from the handsome sporty figure he once had been. Harvey had never seen Powell when he was healthy, because he was already in a serious decline when first brought to Drake. But John's wife, Patricia, had shown Harvey a picture.

The devil-may-care young man with the luxuriant mustache had been reduced to an object of pity.

Annette House, the nurse on duty, conducted the staff briefing. She told Harvey, "Powell's condition has deteriorated further. You know he was already listed as critical." Harvey nodded, and Annette continued. "Dr. Verma said he's not going to make it this time. It would be futile to take him back to the University of Cincinnati Medical Center again. Mrs. Powell has agreed he won't be returned for more aggressive treatment."

Harvey thought, "Why don't they just let him die? That's what I would want if I were in his condition." But he kept his thoughts to himself.

"Keep him as comfortable as possible. Use that skin cream to ease the irritation on his bottom."

"I don't think he even feels it. I looked in on him already this morning, and he's just there, if you know what I mean."

"I know. But Dr. Verma said to keep giving him the antibiotics through his IV to combat his pneumonia and septicemia. It's not up to us to decide when to let go. When an emergency arises, and it will, we won't use any heroic measures to prolong his life."

Harvey knew when to shut up. But he didn't agree with the instructions. John Powell would want to die, if he was capable of any thought. Patricia Powell must want him to die and get it over with, though of course she wouldn't say so.

Duncan was right. He had compassion. And Harvey had the solution in his pocket.

Powell was a mere forty-four years old, younger than most of the patients Harvey cared for at Drake. He had sustained severe head injuries in a motorcycle accident on July 8, 1986, and had been taken to the emergency room of the University of Cincinnati Medical Center (UCMC). It had been a hot day, and he had been riding without a helmet.

At UCMC he underwent a left-side craniotomy for removal of a hematoma and a left partial frontal and parietal lobectomy. He was transferred to Drake on August 27, 1986, in a more-or-less unresponsive state.

He showed modest improvement during the next five months at Drake. Although he never fully regained consciousness, he was sometimes able to open his eyes and show a degree of responsiveness to visitors.

On January 30, 1987, he suffered a pulmonary embolism and respiratory tract infection and was transferred to UCMC for treatment. He was returned to Drake on February 9, but three days later was found to be in shock precipitated by blood poisoning. He was transferred back to UCMC. There he was classified "no code." That meant there would be no efforts to resuscitate should that occasion arise. His sepsis responded to antibiotics, and he was transferred to Drake for the third time on February 23, 1987.

Upon his return to Drake, Powell was unresponsive to Dr. Verma's questions and did not follow any simple commands. Dr. Verma concluded that the prognosis for improvement was poor and that recurrent infections and other physical problems were to be expected.

These pessimistic expectations were borne out on March 3, as Powell had several seizures, for which he was treated with Valium. Tests showed recurrence of pneumonia and blood poisoning. Both infections failed to respond to aggressive treatment with antibiotics.

On this morning, following the briefing, Harvey went about his routine duties of patient care. Shortly before eight o'clock, he reached Powell's room. Powell was comatose. Harvey pulled the curtain around Powell's bed.

After listening for a moment to be sure no one was approaching, Harvey removed the cap from his vial of cyanide and poured half the contents into Powell's gastric feeding tube. He capped the vial and returned it to his pocket.

Powell's reaction was almost instantaneous. He appeared to struggle for breath, then twitched once and was still. Harvey hurried to the nurse's station and told Annette House that Powell was dying. Since Powell was "no code," she raised no alarm. After all, his death was expected. She went to C-300 with Harvey for a quick check to confirm that Powell was dead, returned to her station, and called Dr. Sarkar, staff physician on duty. Dr. Sarkar confirmed the time of death at 8:05 A.M. on March 7, 1987.

Harvey went to the staff restroom, poured the rest of the contents of the vial in the toilet, flushed the toilet, and rinsed the vial at the sink. He went about his duties with his other patients.

Later, Annette found him and instructed him to assist in preparing Powell's body for the morgue. He removed all of the tubes, including the gastric tube, and disposed of them in the trash.

Patricia Powell was called and given the news. Asked whether she wanted to come to see him, she declined. She consented to an autopsy.

On the death summary, Dr. Sarkar reported the cause of death:

1. *Pneumonia.*
2. *Recurrent pulmonary embolism—immediate cause.*
3. *Head injury with status post craniotomy for evacuation of subdural hematoma, resulting in unresponsive state of mind, totally dependent for all ADT* [Activities of Daily Living].

Harvey knew that because Powell's hospitalization was originally the result of an accident, his death was technically a "coroner's case." That meant there would be an autopsy performed. Harvey didn't know Patricia had given permission, but if she hadn't, the hospital would have obtained a court order. Harvey wasn't worried, because he knew that in such a routine and obvious case the autopsy would be a formality. Although cyanide was detectable if laboratory tests were performed on samples taken before embalming, there would be no reason to submit samples for such a test.

That night Donald performed an abbreviated ceremony. He told Duncan, "I did Powell."

3. A Disturbing Discovery

Dr. Lee D. Lehman, forensic pathologist, detected the murder of John Powell through circumstances that could occur only in real life. The coincidences that led to his discovery would be unacceptable in fiction.

No one meeting Dr. Lehman for the first time would associate this stocky, affable, round-faced man with the grisly business of cutting into dead bodies. In his white lab coat, he looked more like a friendly neighborhood pharmacist or a high-school biology teacher. Perhaps one could picture him dissecting a frog in front of a class of giggling teenagers.

Lee Lehman grew up on a farm in Indiana, expecting that he would eventually take over management of the family farm. But first he went to Bluffton College, where he became interested in chemistry, receiving a B.A. degree with a double major in chemistry and mathematics. Fascinated by research, he continued his education at Indiana University, obtaining a Ph.D. in chemistry, specializing in biochemistry.

As he was nearing completion of his Ph.D. studies, Lehman decided to continue at Indiana for a medical degree. During his third year of medical school he selected pathology as a specialty. Upon receiving his M.D., he entered a four-year residency at the South Bend Medical Foundation.

While he was in his residency, the highly publicized Chicago poisonings by cyanide injected into Tylenol capsules stimulated interest in the detection of cyanide. Dr. Lehman undertook a study of the sensitivity of pathologists and morgue attendants to the odor of cyanide. Undetected cyanide could pose a hazard to such workers during an autopsy.

Cyanides react with water, even with moisture from the air, to produce hydrogen cyanide (cyanic acid), a deadly gas with a characteristic odor usually described as smelling like bitter almonds. Of course, few people have smelled bitter almonds, so most people wouldn't identify the gas if they smelled it.

Furthermore, Dr. Lehman found that the ability to detect the odor is selective; to about a fifth of the population the compound is odorless. Dr. Lehman is one of the eighty percent who can smell cyanide, and one of the far smaller group of people who know the odor and can identify it.

After completion of his residency in the fall of 1986, Dr. Lehman joined the Hamilton County, Ohio, coroner's staff as a Fellow in Forensic Pathology. His duties included performing autopsies. In accord with his junior status, he was likely to be working on weekends.

On Sunday morning, March 8, 1987 he was scheduled to perform an autopsy on John Powell, whose body had been delivered from Drake Hospital on Saturday. He expected a routine procedure. He knew that Powell had died after a prolonged hospitalization during which there had never been much hope of recovery.

Dr. Lehman fully expected to confirm the attending physician's report that a pulmonary embolism following pneumonia was the cause of death. All the hospital records were consistent with that conclusion.

The only reason for the involvement of the coroner's office was the Ohio law requiring that an autopsy be performed on any accident victim. Since Powell's hospitalization stemmed from a motorcycle accident, even though that occurred nine months earlier, the law was applicable.

Dr. Lehman dressed in scrubs and put on a protective rubberized gown. Entering the brilliantly lit, but chilly, autopsy room at the morgue, he donned a facemask and rubber gloves. His diener (morgue assistant), similarly attired, had placed Powell's body on the stainless steel dissecting table with an identifying tag attached to the big toe of the right foot.

The diener photographed the body, washed it, drew a diagram of scars and identifying marks, and photographed those. Meanwhile, Dr. Lehman examined the body visually, recording notes on a form attached to a clipboard.

Because there was no suspicion about Powell's death, no police officer was present to observe.

When the preliminaries were complete, Dr. Lehman took a scalpel and made the standard autopsy incision, a Y-shaped cut from each shoulder to the pit of the stomach, continuing down and through the pubic region. With a pair of long-handled clippers, he cut through the ribs and removed the front plate to provide access to the chest cavity. Removing the organs in turn, he handed each organ to the diener to be weighed and saved for examination. As he worked, he dictated his observations into a foot-controlled recorder linked to a lapel microphone.

When he opened the stomach, the routine autopsy suddenly took on an entirely different character. Lehman smelled what was to him the unmistakable odor of cyanide. He motioned to the diener. "Smell this . . . don't get too close!"

The diener sniffed. "What is it?"

"What does it smell like to you?"

"I don't recognize it. Sorta musty or burnt."

"How about bitter almonds?"

"I never smelled any."

Lehman shrugged. "You should have been taught that one, for your own safety. That's cyanide. And it's deadly. The odor of bitter almonds is the generally accepted description. Remember it. And avoid it."

Dr. Lehman took samples of blood and all fluids in the body cavity and urine in the bladder. He examined the contents of the stomach and took samples.

Although he had a strong indication of death by poisoning, Dr. Lehman meticulously completed the autopsy. He sectioned each organ for visual examination and took a tissue sample for further microscopic examination and laboratory tests.

The diener sliced across the top of the scalp and pulled flaps forward and backward to provide access to the skull. With a surgical saw, he sliced off the top of the skull and extracted the brain for Dr. Lehman's examination. Dr. Lehman confirmed the fractures from the motorcycle accident, and the brain showed the expected damage from the accident and subsequent surgery. The diener photographed the brain.

When Dr. Lehman had completed his examination of the organs and had taken the necessary samples, the diener placed the organs in a plastic bag and returned them to the body cavity. He sewed up the incision loosely, because the mortician would have to open it again.

Dr. Lehman sent a blood sample to the toxicological laboratory to be tested for cyanide. The results were positive. Cyanide was present. John Powell had not died a natural death.

Upon receiving the laboratory results, Dr. Lehman notified the Hamilton County coroner, Dr. Frank Cleveland. Because Lehman suspected homicide, he sent samples to an independent laboratory for confirmation of the analysis. He was dismayed and incredulous when the reported results were negative for all samples. No cyanide.

Another pathologist might have accepted that report. Powell's death would have been recorded as resulting from a pulmonary embolism caused by pneumonia, and the only legal questions would have related to the accident that had initially sent him to the hospital.

Dr. Lehman's training in chemistry, however, would not allow him to accept those findings. He had the tests repeated on samples of both blood and stomach contents in the laboratory attached to the coroner's office and obtained positive results.

He knew that the test for cyanide involves a gaseous diffusion step in which the sample is treated with acid to release hydrogen cyanide gas that is absorbed into an alkaline medium. The solution thus obtained is treated with a reagent that reacts with the cyanide to produce a characteristic color. (The word "cyanide" comes from a Greek word for dark blue.) The intensity of the color varies with the concentration of the cyanide. The analyst measures the intensity with a color spectrometer calibrated against standard samples to indicate the concentration.

He called the outside laboratory. "There's something wrong with those tests for cyanide. We've checked our analysis. Cyanide is present. I'm sending you another set of samples. Are you sure your colorimeter was calibrated correctly?"

"We'll check it. Send us the samples."

The outside laboratory reported that the calibration was indeed in error. The coroner's toxicology laboratory's findings were confirmed.

As Dr. Lehman said later, "Cyanide does not exist naturally in the human body. And as soon as I made my incision, I knew foul play was the likely cause of death."

It was time to involve the Cincinnati Police Department. John Powell's death was a homicide.

4. A Murder Case for a Public Defender

Hamilton County Coroner Dr. Frank Cleveland called Lt. Bill Fletcher, commander of the Cincinnati Homicide/Rape Squad, for a meeting to discuss John Powell's death. Because Drake Hospital is situated within the city limits of Cincinnati, a homicide there fell under Cincinnati's police jurisdiction.

In addition to Dr. Cleveland and Lt. Fletcher, the meeting was attended by Dr. Cleveland's assistant, Carol Martera, and police officers Sgt. Paul Morgan, John Jay, Ron Camden, and Jim Lawson. Dr. Cleveland and Ms. Martera presented Dr. Lehman's findings from the autopsy and subsequent laboratory tests and provided details about Powell's medical history leading up to his death.

Lt. Fletcher launched an immediate investigation. He assigned Morgan, Jay, Camden, and Lawson to the case.

The police first checked the possibility that Powell's food supply had been accidentally contaminated. Knowing that Powell had been receiving his nourishment from a gastric tube, they reviewed medical records to determine whether any other patients with gastric tubes had become ill recently and tested the supplement on hand for cyanide.

When these results were negative, they knew Powell had been murdered. They investigated simultaneously motive and opportunity. Powell's widow, Patricia, appeared to have a strong motive for wishing his death. Powell was semi-comatose, and although his condition was deteriorating and the doctors had no hope of his recovery, he could linger in that condition for a long time. His medical insurance had run out. The medical bills were piling up. He had a life insurance policy with his wife as beneficiary.

The police interviewed Patricia Powell three different times. She agreed to take a polygraph test. The results of the test cleared her of suspicion. None of his family or friends turned out to be likely suspects.

The police compiled from hospital records a list of everyone who had contact with him during his last few days, including a log of his visitors. They conducted thirty-five interviews. Among those interviewed was a nurse who had worked in a foreign hospital and said she believed in euthanasia. She convinced them that she had nothing to do with Powell's death, but her comments initiated the thought that his death might have been a mercy killing.

During these interviews, Donald Harvey's name came up. Someone mentioned that he'd worked at the Veterans Administration hospital in Cincinnati and had left under questionable circumstances. A check of his employment records verified that he'd worked at the VA hospital, but there was no indication that anything was amiss. Follow-up interviews at the VA hospital were inconclusive.

It was reported that he'd been allowed to resign after a pistol was found in his gym bag. He had not been charged with any violation, apparently because of procedural errors. (See chapters 12 and 24.) The administrators at Drake were not aware of those circumstances or of additional suspicions uncovered by the police.

Harvey had worked in the pathology department at the VA hospital, and one of his duties had been to take organs to be incinerated after tests were completed. A rumor had circulated that instead of incinerating the organs, he had given some to a man by the name of Thomas Hudson* [ficticious] for use in satanic rituals.

Hudson had been convicted of a murder involving a legless corpse. He was suspected of cutting off the legs for a ceremonial sacrifice, but it was subsequently determined that he had removed the legs because rigor had set in and the body wouldn't fit into the trunk of the car used to transport it.

The rumor of Harvey's connection to Hudson was never substantiated and was apparently false, but the coincidence aroused Camden's and Lawson's interest in Harvey as a suspect in Powell's death.

While Harvey was not aware of the specific attention of the police to his employment at the VA hospital, he knew of the investigation at Drake. He undertook to dispose of evidence from his trailer. He took the skull to a dump and buried it in a mound of garbage. He took his cache of cyanide and dumped it into the Great Miami River. He also had a jar of arsenic, which he mixed into a can of paint. He had been carrying a vial of cyanide solution with the intention of committing suicide if he were caught, but he disposed of that also.

He started planning to flee if he came under closer scrutiny. He developed a plan of finding someone who resembled him, killing that person, putting his own jewelry on him, and burning the body in his car.

He thought he had found a suitable victim and persuaded him to have a blood test, ostensibly to ensure that he was not HIV positive before having sex with him. He actually wanted to check his blood type. The potential victim was B+ and Harvey is A+, so he knew his deception would fail. He abandoned the plan.

Beginning to feel cornered, he withdrew $1,500 from his bank account and began carrying that cash in order to facilitate a getaway. Panic was now distorting his thoughts. He failed to crystallize any idea of how he would travel or where he could go.

Learning that hospital employees were being scheduled to take polygraph tests, he obtained a book about lie detectors from the library and studied it with the intention of learning how to foil the test. He agreed to take the test, but on the scheduled date called and canceled, saying he was sick. He was rescheduled.

When he finally went in for the test, the polygraph operator explained the procedure. Harvey would be connected to an apparatus that measured physiological symptoms of his reactions during a question-and-answer session. Some of the questions would be innocuous ones to measure a base line of his responses. Some questions would relate to the case but would be ones expected to cause no unusual reactions from him. Others would be pertinent and might pose a threat. Should he lie, the apparatus would measure a change in physiological reactions that would indicate he felt stress. The test was voluntary. The police could not force him to take it.

Harvey refused the test.

(Years later, a psychologist expressed an opinion that Harvey's psychological makeup was such that he probably could have taken the polygraph test and lied without detection. He wouldn't have the normal reactions. Harvey now agrees that he probably would have passed the test.)

Jim Lawson asked, "Well, if you don't want to take the test, do you want to talk with us?"

Harvey agreed. They went to an interview room in the temporary head-quarters of the homicide squad. This room was on the sixth floor of the Alms & Doepke Building, a former department store in downtown Cincinnati converted to municipal use. The room had a sound system that allowed the conversation to be monitored from an adjacent room. The purpose of the setup was to insure the safety of the investigating officers and to use in training interviewers. Since both Lawson and Camden were experienced interrogators, the training aspect was not needed, but other officers could listen in.

The interview lasted about five hours, with frequent rest breaks. For some reason of his own, Harvey liked Jim Lawson and responded well to his questioning. Perhaps Harvey was responding to Lawson's casual, friendly manner. Lawson appeared relaxed as he sprawled in a chair with his legs stretched out. His unruly sandy hair added to that impression. They were soon calling each other Jim and Don.

Ron Camden was somewhat more formal. He sat erectly and gazed intensely at Harvey. His dark hair stayed neatly in place. He leaned forward whenever he asked a question. Harvey did not like Camden and frequently ignored his questions, although he would answer the same questions repeated by Jim. When asked later about the interrogation, Lt. Fletcher said that Jim and Ron did not deliberately employ a "good cop, bad cop" technique, but that's how it worked out.

Jim Lawson led Harvey through a discussion of the John Powell case. Finally, Harvey said, "Jim, I did it. I put cyanide in his G-tube."

"Why?"

"I felt sorry for him, and for his family. It's what I would want somebody to do for me if I were in that condition." Donald told Lawson that Powell reminded him of his own father.

"Have you done that for anyone else?"

"No."

Jim had him describe exactly what he had done.

Upon further questioning, Harvey said that he obtained the cyanide from the laboratory at Drake and told Jim where to find the jar. The police retrieved the jar of cyanide but determined that it probably was not the source of the cyanide Harvey had used. That finding was important, because it weakened the credibility of Harvey's confession.

After some more conversation, Lawson asked again, "Have you been responsible for any more deaths of patients?"

"I don't remember. Sometimes I think I'm two different people, and I don't know what the other one does."

Lawson terminated the interview, fearing that Harvey was trying to set up a foundation for an insanity defense. Although Lawson's reasons were logical at that point in the investigation, the subsequent course of the case could have been greatly different had he pursued that issue.

Police charged Harvey with aggravated (first-degree) murder on Monday, April 6, 1987.

The next day, the story competed with an account of the Cincinnati Reds' opening day for space on the front page of the *Cincinnati Enquirer*. The Reds came from behind to beat Montreal 11–5. Eric Davis went three-for-three.

Under a headline reading, "Orderly charged in poisoning: Death possibly a mercy killing," the story began: "John Powell was a helpless invalid at Drake Hospital when someone killed him with a dose of cyanide last month, Cincinnati police said Monday."

After reporting that the poisoning was discovered through a routine autopsy conducted because Powell's hospitalization was the result of an accident, the story continued: "The discovery prompted Coroner Frank Cleveland to order autopsies for all deaths at Drake since then. . . . As of Monday, no other suspicious deaths had been discovered . . ."

The article included the information: "Drake, a county-owned, long-term center . . . averages two deaths a week."

Jailed to await trial, Harvey asked that the public defender's office provide a lawyer, since he did not have the money to pay for his defense. The public defender provides an attorney from his own staff if the charge is a misdemeanor, but for more serious crimes, the judge selects an attorney from a list kept by the public defender's office.

That was the beginning of my involvement with Donald Harvey. Hamilton County Court of Common Pleas Judge Ralph Winkler, the presiding criminal judge for that month, appointed me as Harvey's defense attorney. Judge Winkler owed me a favor because I had withdrawn from an earlier case in his court at his request when he wanted to appoint a different attorney. Serving as defense attorney in a murder trial is considered a plum, both because of the visibility and because the fees are higher than for lesser crimes.

I was formerly an assistant prosecutor, working under Art Ney, the Hamilton County prosecutor. After leaving Ney's office, I had become a specialist in criminal defense work. My clients tended to be at the lower levels of society, charged with auto theft, prostitution, assault, trafficking in drugs, or attempted rape.

I was intimately familiar with the machinery and personnel of the criminal justice system in Hamilton County, Ohio. Harvey's was just another case, interesting mainly for the mercy-killing angle that might attract public attention.

My appointment was no big deal at the time. Judge Winkler didn't even tell me about it himself. I was informed of my appointment by a member of the public defender's office.

I didn't have an opportunity to get to the North Building of the Hamilton County Justice Center to meet my new client until late in the morning. I was full of curiosity. People in the courthouse were already talking about the case. Who and what was this mercy killer? I had never been involved in a trial of a mercy killer and knew of no previous case. My adrenaline was already flowing with the thought of such a prospect.

Harvey was being held in the psychiatric unit, reserved for inmates appearing unstable or considered possibly suicidal. I wondered about that. I'd had no inkling that my client's sanity was questioned.

Dr. Nancy Schmidtgoessling, the psychologist heading the Court Psychiatric Unit, had a reputation for unbiased professionalism. She was administering the Minnesota Multiphasic Personality Inventory (MMPI) to him. This test consists of a set of 567 empirically tested questions to which emotionally disturbed subjects respond differently from normal people. Harvey's test was interrupted so that he could meet with me.

My visit with Harvey was very brief. There was no place for us to sit, and I felt uncomfortable trying to talk with a new client while standing in an open area with other people milling around.

On that day when I first met my client, I found him to be like a cornered animal—wild-eyed, agitated, frightened. He babbled incoherently, and I hardly understood his story. I could understand then why they had put him in the psychiatric unit. Years later, Harvey explained to me that he had been taking Deseryl, prescribed by his psychiatrist, but had been instructed not to take the medicine before his police interview. Harvey claimed that he was suffering from withdrawal at the time of that first interview. He recalls practically nothing of that meeting.

Because I was involved in another case, I had only a few minutes to spend with Harvey then. I gave him my card and instructed him to talk to no one about the case in my absence. I told him he could talk with the doctors and nurses, but not about the case.

I returned to the justice center late that afternoon. This time we had a place to meet. Harvey was brought in and slid into a bench facing me across a small table. He did not appear so fearful. He moved with more comfort, and his smile indicated recognition. I told him that we were going to be a team and I felt it was time for us to get to know each other. I didn't realize then how much of an understatement that would turn out to be. I asked him how his day had gone and checked to make sure he had not talked with anyone about the case.

I told Harvey that I had been an assistant prosecutor, because I knew that history upset some potential clients.

"That doesn't bother me."

When I asked him for some of his history, he sat straighter and talked freely of growing up in Kentucky. He told me about his mother and his sister. Then he said that he was a Vietnam War veteran.

I became more alert. Here was something I could use to impress a jury or perhaps in a plea for mitigation. "Did you see action in Vietnam?"

I'm sure my body language encouraged him. He leaned forward, and his voice softened. His speech slowed as he said, "Yes. I was part of a special squad, a medical unit whose job was to find dead Vietnamese and remove their hearts for studies of cholesterol."

I leaned back. "I never heard of such a study."

"It was top secret. There were only seven of us in the unit."

"Give me the names of the other men in the unit, so I can verify this information."

"They are all dead. I was the only survivor."

I made a mental note to check that out and changed the subject.

I repeated my instructions about not discussing the case with anyone and told him I would be back.

I asked Dr. Schmidtgoessling about the results of the MMPI. She told me that Harvey had given responses that indicated he was lying. Some of the questions in the MMPI are designed to trap subjects who are trying to fool the test into indicating mental unbalance. Schmidtgoessling urged me to tell my client to stop "trying to be crazy."

Harvey denied trying to skew the results, but when he was retested several weeks later, he still gave invalid responses. Questioned again much later about this test, he said that he was not trying to fool the test, but he didn't take it seriously and was "just playing around." He said he took this test six times altogether for different psychologists and did decide to have some fun with them, screwing up the results, but not trying to fake any particular analysis.

Two days later, Harvey seemed much more rational. I found him cooperative, intelligent, and willing to provide a wealth of detail.

I learned he had no criminal record of any kind in Ohio.

I found his mercy-killing story so credible that I started to build his defense on that angle. Self-defense was obviously not a possibility, because Powell was a helpless invalid. An alibi seemed unlikely, because the hospital records showed Harvey was working that shift. It did not seem reasonable to think that his confession could be rejected, but I filed a routine motion to suppress. I hoped to hold the damage to a manslaughter verdict with a sentence of a few years at most. With real luck, we might even win acquittal.

I undertook to verify the story about his service in Vietnam. His sister told me that he had been in the Air Force, but the most distant land he had visited was California. When I confronted him, Donald admitted the lie and attributed it to the medication he had been taking.

The story was a strange echo of a story Donald's father once told about his military service, claiming that he had been assigned to exhume the bodies of American soldiers buried in Korea in order for them to be returned home for burial. That story was obviously false, because Donald's father's service had been during World War II. He never had any involvement with the Korean War.

Based on this story and my own observations when I first saw my client, I thought that sanity could be an issue. First, I filed with the court a Suggestion of Incompetency, a document whereby the attorney informs the court that he believes the client to be in such a mental state that he is incapable of assisting in the preparation of his defense. The law will not proceed with prosecution of an accused who is incompetent.

I also filed a plea of Not Guilty by Reason of Insanity (NGRI). In Ohio, this defense requires that the case meet two criteria:

The defendant must have a mental disease or psychosis, such as schizophrenia, or a mental defect (retardation or brain injury).

The crime must be a result of that disease or defect and the defendant either could not resist the urge to commit the crime or did not know the act was wrong.

Roger Fisher, a clinical psychologist, examined Harvey for the court. His report stated:

"In my opinion, on March 7, 1987, Mr. Harvey was free of any emotional disease or defect of the mind so substantial or significant that it would have impaired his reason. I believe he was fully aware of the difference between right and wrong and was able to conform his conduct to the dictates of the law, if he had chosen to do so. In fact, I believe he was aware that placing cyanide in the feeding tube of a patient would have resulted in that patient's death and that it was wrong to do so. He even knew he would be caught. However, I believe Mr. Harvey engaged in this action in order to strengthen his own motivation to commit suicide."

Dr. Schmidtgoessling reported her findings. She concluded that Harvey had a history of depression stemming from his childhood experiences but that he was not and had never been psychotic.

The competency hearing was scheduled for May 26. Based on the reports and my private discussion with Dr. Schmidtgoessling, I concluded that it would be futile to challenge the findings in a cross-examination. I offered to waive the hearing and stipulate the reports. The court ruled that Harvey was competent to stand trial.

Harvey was charged with one count of murder. If convicted, he faced a sentence of fifteen years to life, with eligibility for parole in ten years.

The case against Harvey was strong, and I was certain that a judge would find him guilty. A rule of thumb in the legal community is that if you have a strong defense on legal issues, you try the case to a judge, but that was certainly not Harvey's situation. He could demand trial by jury. A conviction by a jury requires a unanimous decision. If I could get even one juror to accept the idea that this was a mercy killing, he might get a mistrial and even a dismissal.

An alternative was to plea bargain, manslaughter instead of murder. For manslaughter, the judge has a wide discretionary range. The minimum sentence would be five to twenty-five years, and the maximum would be eight to twenty-five years. Many judges are willing to make a decision on the sentence in advance and inform the attorney, so the defendant can make an informed decision about a plea bargain.

I discussed the possibility of a plea bargain with the prosecutor. I used the argument that a conviction in a jury trial is never a sure thing, that the state would be saved the time and expense of a trial, and that Powell's family would be spared the anguish of the testimony. Harvey had agreed for me to try this route. Although the prosecutor's response was no, I felt that was just the beginning of a bargaining position.

But suddenly, the apparently straightforward case took a dramatic turn anticipated by neither the prosecutor nor the defense.

5. A Dramatic Newscast

Arraignment of Donald Harvey, charged with murder in the death of John Powell, rated coverage on the local evening news. Dr. Lehman's discovery that Powell had been poisoned with cyanide had already aroused public interest, and the suggestion that Powell's death might be a mercy killing had reinforced that interest.

Pat Minarcin, anchor for WCPO-TV evening news, sensed that the story might be even bigger.

After a reporter had given an account of the court action, Minarcin asked whether the police were investigating the possibility that Harvey had been responsible for any other deaths at Drake Hospital. The reporter answered no; they had told her it would be futile. Cyanide could not be detected after embalming.

Although Minarcin didn't question that answer on the air, his instincts as an investigative reporter were alerted. Did the law enforcement officials think a killer who had used cyanide once was limited to that one poison—or couldn't have killed others by a completely different method? What was unique about John Powell that caused Harvey to decide to end the suffering for him and not others?

The police and the prosecutor's office had closed the investigation only two days after obtaining Harvey's confession. They could claim efficiency—crime discovered, perpetrator identified, confession obtained, time to get on to other cases. But Minarcin wondered. Were they apathetic because Drake was a county hospital and most of the patients on that floor were expected to die there? Could there be another, even more sinister, reason not to probe more deeply?

Minarcin had never accepted the concept that his role as an anchor was to package and present to the public the news that was delivered to him. In his ten years with the Associated Press as a writer, reporter, editor, and bureau chief, he had learned that digging into the background of a news story could yield unexpected expansion. When he was editor of *Pennsylvania Illustrated* magazine in Harrisburg, his in-depth coverage of the Three Mile Island nuclear power plant disaster had earned the magazine a Distinguished Service Award from Sigma Delta Chi, the Society of Professional Journalists. He considered he had a duty to look behind the surface of a news story for the more significant story that might be overlooked.

His instincts about the story of John Powell's death at Drake Hospital were confirmed four days after the broadcast. He received an anonymous telephone call from a nurse at Drake Hospital. She said he was right to question dropping the investigation. "There is something going on here, and our supervisors won't do anything about it." She gave him a list of thirteen other patients she thought Harvey might have killed.

Minarcin asked for her name, but she refused to give it. She was obviously afraid of job repercussions. She did agree, however, to call him again the following night and provide more information.

When she called, she had another nurse on the line to add her support to the accusation. They told him that they had gone to their nursing supervisor, Daisy Key, several times before Harvey's arrest to tell her of their suspicions about him. At first, she had ignored them. Then she ordered them to keep quiet. The nurses added three more names to the list of suspected victims. Minarcin asked for some proof, but his callers said they were unable to do more. They again refused to give their names, but they agreed to call him again.

A day passed with no contact. Minarcin waited anxiously, hesitating to take any action that might alert the hospital supervisors and further frighten his informers. As preparation for the next call, whenever it came, he obtained the death certificates of the sixteen patients on his list. The records seemed to be in order, and none indicated any suspicion that the deaths were not natural.

The following evening, Minarcin was at the studio preparing to go on the air in thirty minutes, when he received a call. This time, five of the hospital staff were on the line, supporting the accusation that Harvey had been responsible for multiple deaths at Drake. They refused to identify themselves or to provide any more information. Minarcin tried to arrange a meeting, but they were adamant. They were seriously concerned about the situation, but they had done all they dared to do.

Minarcin sensed an opportunity that might be gone forever if he lost contact now. He put his own job on the line. "Look, what if I just dropped everything right now and came out there and saw the five of you alone?" He held his breath while they discussed the offer among themselves.

He heaved a sigh of relief when they agreed, but now he had another problem. He was due on the air in twenty minutes in a format that called for two anchors. With no time to find a replacement, his co-anchor would have to fly alone. The camera crew would need to scrap their plan and improvise. Minarcin's boss, Jack Cahalan, news director for the station, reluctantly agreed to his defection.

Minarcin rushed to his meeting. The five were still there. Perhaps his action in skipping his newscast influenced them, for as they talked, they began to open up.

He learned their fears about their jobs were not paranoia. The day after Harvey's arrest, Jan Taylor, the chief administrator of Drake Hospital, had called a meeting of the staff members who worked on Ward C. He told them that the hospital had conducted an internal investigation and found no indication that Harvey had killed anyone else. He said the police investigation had been thorough and confirmed the findings of the internal investigation. He asked the staff to refrain from discussing the matter among themselves and ordered them not to talk to reporters.

The five described for Minarcin the occasions that had aroused their suspicions of Harvey. They provided names and dates and told of rebuffs by their supervisors when they reported his behavior. They increased Minarcin's list of suspicious deaths to thirty-three.

Armed with this information, Minarcin launched his own intensive probe of deaths at Drake Hospital. Because Drake was a public institution, he was able to obtain official records from the hospital. He gradually developed additional sources of information within the hospital, and they provided more documents. He became convinced that the accusations were true; Donald Harvey had been systematically killing patients at the hospital and getting away with it. But Minarcin lacked proof. He couldn't go on the air with what he had.

Minarcin's activities came to the attention of Jan Taylor. Taylor was certain that Minarcin was obtaining information from staff members in addition to the public documents he requested. Taylor undertook to discover those sources and plug the leaks. General staff meetings became more frequent.

Hospital officials attempted to discredit Minarcin with character assassination. At the staff meetings, they denounced him as a "sensationalist," claiming that he was blatantly trying to improve his program's ratings at the expense of the hospital. Minarcin's inside sources reported these efforts to him, adding to his conviction that the hospital had something to hide.

A breakthrough came one Sunday afternoon as Minarcin sifted and sorted the documents spread over his dining-room table. He was making charts of death rates on each ward, arranged by dates. When he added another dimension, Harvey's work schedule, a pattern emerged. And when he compared that pattern with the anecdotal data supplied by his inside sources, the correspondence could not be attributed to chance or coincidence. He had the handle on his story.

Yes, he had a story.

But could he put it on the air? Harvey had confessed to aggravated murder of John Powell and had been charged with the crime; but he had not come to trial. There was at least a reasonable chance that he might be found not guilty or guilty of a lesser crime, because of characterization of his act as a mercy killing. Minarcin's story might prejudice his case, with legal repercussions for Minarcin and the television station. The hospital and the hospital administrators were sure to challenge the report and perhaps to file suits.

Minarcin approached me and told me he was working on a story suggesting that Harvey had been responsible for multiple deaths at Drake. He asked for a comment. I responded with irritation, "No comment," thinking that Minarcin was trying to manufacture a sensation and increase the program's ratings at the expense of my client. It had never occurred to me as I prepared Harvey's defense to ask if he had killed anyone else at the hospital.

I tried to return to the work that had been interrupted by Minarcin's call, but I was unable to do so.

Haunted by the call, I walked the two blocks to the justice center to warn my client that the story would likely appear on the news. Believing that John Powell had been his only victim, I felt obligated to warn Harvey of the upcoming broadcast and also wanted to put the matter to rest in my own mind. Harvey was pleased to see me, and we engaged first in light conversation. I could warm more to Harvey than to my usual clients, because he was more intelligent and articulate than the petty criminals whose cases were more often assigned to me as a public defender.

I gave Harvey a little lecture, explaining that I could not completely protect his interests if he were not truthful with me. I told him what I had learned from Minarcin. Explaining the privacy of the attorney-client privilege, I ended with the question, "Have you killed more than just John Powell?"

Without hesitation, but almost inaudibly, Harvey replied, "Yes."

Alarm bells began sounding in my head as I realized I had just fallen into uncharted territory. Moments before, relaxed and at ease, I was representing a confessed mercy killer. With one simple word, realization came that I was looking into the eyes of a serial killer.

I had no experience with the term, having only read about serial killers in books and sensational news stories. I wondered, "What does one do when intimately involved with one, and how serial is a serial killer? Are two deaths enough to make one a serial killer? Is there a limit?" For whatever reason, I assumed we were talking about two or three deaths.

I shifted to the edge of my chair. "How many people have you killed?"

Harvey's response was immediate, "I can't tell you."

Irritated, I raised my voice. "I just told you, I can't help you if you don't cooperate with me."

My outburst evoked a defensive response. "It's not that I don't want to tell you, but I can only estimate."

The word "estimate," like the sounds of an arcade game, alerted me to prepare for a shock. It was clear that people do not estimate two or three deaths.

"Five?" I asked. "Ten?"

Harvey hung his head and shook it. "More."

Chilled by apprehension, I groped for words to elicit an answer I knew I'd rather not hear. I recalled a technique once used by Common Pleas Judge Crush. I had been in his courtroom when he was trying to determine whether a defendant had stolen enough trinkets to reach a value sufficient for his crime to be classified as a felony instead of a misdemeanor. The defendant said he couldn't remember the number of items, so the judge asked him to state a number that he was certain was the top limit. The defendant kept revising his number upward under repeated questioning but finally stopped at a figure that was still well below the requirement. The judge and the attorneys had a good laugh afterward in the judge's chambers, but I remembered the incident.

I used Judge Crush's technique. "Okay, Donald, pick a number in your mind that you know the number of deaths could not go beyond."

It seemed like an hour that Harvey's dark eyes never left mine, and the silence enveloped both of us. I finally broke the silence and asked if he had a figure.

Harvey's only response was a slight nod of his head. I asked for the number. The word was whispered, but distinctly, "Seventy."

Although the conversation continued for forty-five minutes more, I have no recollection of what was said. The number, "70," blinked on and off in my mind like a neon sign.

Leaving that brick institution, I walked for blocks trying to clear my mind and gain some grasp of the situation. I tried to convince myself that it was a lie and a bad joke on me. But how could I explain Minarcin's phone call that he believed there had been more than one death at Drake Hospital? If Harvey were lying, then why such an outrageous figure as seventy? The entire situation was now surreal.

Then the question was what I should do with the information even if the number were two? Two or more deaths in the state of Ohio qualify one to ride "Old Sparky," the electric chair.

Section 2929.04 of the Ohio Revised Code states:

"(A) Imposition of the death penalty for aggravated murder is precluded unless one or more of the following is specified in the indictment or count in the indictment pursuant to section 2941.14 of the Revised Code and proved beyond a reasonable doubt:

[Items 1–4 pertain to political assassination; murder for hire; murder to escape detection, apprehension, trial, or punishment for another offense; or murder when under detention or at large after breaking detention.]

(5) Prior to the offense at bar, the offender was convicted of an offense an essential element of which was the purposeful killing of or attempt to kill another, or the offense at bar was part of a course of conduct involving purposeful killing of or attempt to kill two or more persons by the offender."

If Harvey had killed more than one, and the authorities could prove it, the actual number would be of little consequence. If the number really were seventy, how would one deal with that? The simple answer was to keep my mouth shut and hope it would go away.

But what about Minarcin?

I knew I was in a unique situation. Most times a defense attorney is faced with a situation in which the police have already investigated the crime, interrogated witnesses, gathered evidence, and probably talked with the accused. Harvey's case was the opposite. I knew of the crimes, and the law enforcement personnel were completely in the dark.

As a public defender, my primary responsibility had to be to my client. Our system of criminal justice is structured on that basis. The prosecution presents the case against an accused, and the defense seeks to avoid or minimize punishment. In any combat, fairness requires comparable weapons. In a criminal case, those weapons are attorneys. Protection of the public is not the defense attorney's responsibility. But seventy deaths?

Each individual has a time-proven method of dealing with significant issues. Mine had always been talking with peers and friends. To avoid breaching an attorney-client privilege, I asked hypothetical questions, colored the facts, and omitted names; but how could one hypothesize killing seventy people? Who would not know whom I was talking about, or realize it when the story finally surfaced? Even a hypothetical question using the term "killed many people" would elicit questions I could ill afford to raise.

None of my colleagues could possibly have any experience handling a problem of this magnitude. From my wife, I would get sympathy, but no guidance. And I was reluctant to lay the burden of that knowledge upon her.

Walking proved ineffective so I tried driving, with the same result. On a lesser scale, I believed I had some sense of how Daniel felt when the lion entered the arena.

There had to be some higher authority who had an answer, or at least directions.

The next day, as soon as I finished my court cases, I went to the public library and reviewed F. Lee Bailey's book about his handling of the Boston Strangler. Bailey had gone to the police and asked for information about the crime that only the killer would have known, because it had not been made public. Armed with that information, he interrogated his client and found he had that guilty knowledge. Bailey informed the police. I did not appreciate the method used, because I felt Bailey had violated his responsibility to his client, and I had already formed the resolve that I was not going to sacrifice Harvey.

There had to be a way to resolve this satisfactorily, but what was satisfactorily? I returned to Harvey's unit at the justice center. I wasn't sure how I had left my client. A smiling, affable Harvey greeted me without mentioning the devastating news elicited the day before.

Without realizing it, I had begun to form a plan.

I could not leave the issue alone. There were people out there who had reason to suspect that Harvey was a serial killer. The media were already aware of these suspicions, and once the authorities had that information, they would begin searching for that magical second victim.

First, I had to begin protecting my client.

I gave a series of protective instructions to Harvey. He was not to discuss anything about the case with any of the inmates or the guards. All too often an inmate becomes privy to information and immediately seeks to inform the authorities in an attempt to obtain a more favorable outcome of his own case. Harvey assured me there were no notes or written memoranda of the information that he had given me. I warned him that he must not have anything that the authorities could find in his cell. I obtained brief background information, but that was as far as I could approach the subject.

I explained the provisions of the law with regard to the death penalty. Together, Harvey and I reached the conclusion that it was highly improbable the police would not discover at least one more victim, now that the question had been raised.

Harvey fixed me with a wide-eyed stare. "I don't want to die."

"A claim of mercy killing is not going to stand up for multiple deaths."

"But I was relieving them of their misery."

"All of them?"

"Well . . . no." He was silent for a moment. "I don't like it, but what about a plea of insanity?"

"That's already been ruled out."

"Then what?"

"Our only hope is to get the jump on the prosecutor—to use the leverage that only you know who the victims are and negotiate a plea."

"Would I still go to prison?"

I sighed. "Probably for the rest of your life."

"That's better than the electric chair." After a long pause, he continued, "Do what you have to do."

"I need to put pressure of public opinion on the prosecutor for him to bargain. It's risky, and timing will be critical; but I think I need to encourage Minarcin to air his story. I've been stonewalling him, but I think we have a better chance if we get more active—make things happen instead of trying to react to what happens."

Harvey thought a moment. "Okay. So what do I do now?"

"Don't tell anybody anything. Refer everything to me." I sounded more confident than I felt.

It had been a week since Harvey told me of the possibility of seventy more deaths. Seventy? How does one comprehend that number? I needed to talk to someone. Who? If I talked to the wrong person and the story was leaked, Harvey could die. I could not live with that possibility.

I had been raised a Roman Catholic but had not practiced for some time. The seal of confession appealed to me. The Jesuit priests were noted for being broadminded.

I went to Saint Xavier church in downtown Cincinnati at two o'clock. It was a weekday, and the door was locked. I went to the undercroft, and there a woman told me to go up to the church by the inside stairway and the priest would be right up. The beautiful interior of the sanctuary calmed me.

When the priest arrived, I was reassured to find he was elderly. I entered the confessional and began the prayer, but then I stopped. "Father, I am not confessing. I am seeking advice."

"Yes?"

"Does the seal of secrecy still apply?"

He assured me that it did.

The protection of the seal of secrecy gave me a sense of safety. I outlined the situation, giving no names or numbers. I felt relief at just having the opportunity to talk.

When I stopped, he spoke softly, "My son, these items are outside my area of knowledge." I could feel disaster coming. He continued, "God has put the answers in your soul, and you need to search there for the answers. God will give you the direction that you need." He gave me his blessings.

I left the church feeling cheated and disillusioned. I had turned to the church for help, and the priest rejected me. Later, I realized how prophetic his words had been. As I proceeded through the labyrinth of the Harvey case, I found that at each turn I knew which avenue to take. Truly, God led me and the priest's instruction was correct.

Day followed day, and I avidly watched the six o'clock news. Harvey was never mentioned. By the end of the second week, the tension of waiting for the story to drop and Harvey's inquiries as to when the story would appear led me to call Minarcin. It was eleven in the morning. I was told that Minarcin would not be in to work until one o'clock. I didn't leave my name and number; instead I said I'd call back.

At two minutes after one, I called again and Minarcin was put on the phone. He was jovial and friendly until I asked about the story. His mood immediately changed to depression. He explained that the nurses were not willing to waive their demand of anonymity. He could find no other evidence that would permit him to go any further with this story.

His frustration fairly dripped from the telephone, yet unconsciously a plan began to develop. There were too many people who were aware of this situation, and I could not leave it to fate. We needed to use public pressure for action to force the prosecutor to bargain. After a moment's hesitation I responded, "Pat, you need to go forward with this story."

Immediately the tone of Minarcin's voice changed, "What are you saying? You know what he's done, don't you? How many has he killed?"

The barrage of questions and the changed attitude caught me by surprise. I told Minarcin that I could not discuss the matter any further but urged him to go forward with the story. I then hung up.

Minarcin called again the next day. Excitement had returned to his voice. "Are you telling me that I'll find that Harvey was responsible for more deaths at Drake if I just keep digging?"

"I'm saying that that there is more to the story."

"What? What do you know?"

"I can't give you any specifics."

"I need something to go on. Give me a lead. What's your source?"

"I can't tell you."

"Then the source is Harvey, himself, isn't it?"

I didn't reply.

Minarcin tried another tack. "Okay. I understand about privileged communication. But can't you give me a hint, off the record? What do I look for?"

"Just the fact that you are looking will force it out."

"How many people has he killed?"

"He has confessed to killing John Powell."

"Look. You don't want to return a killer to the streets to kill again, do you?"

"My job is to defend Harvey against the one charge of murder."

"You know more than you're telling me. What is it?"

"I've said all I can."

"If there are people out there whose loved one's death was murder, they deserve to know it."

Homicide detectives are familiar with the innate desire in a suspect to "spill his guts." That same desire overwhelmed me, and I was caught in a current leading me in a direction I was not sure I wanted to go. Finally, in an attempt to end the conversation, and yet ensure that Minarcin would follow through with the story, I told him, "Yes, Harvey has admitted to killing more than one person."

"I knew it! Give me some names."

"I can't."

"Well, how many were there?"

"I don't know."

"Was cyanide the only way he killed?"

"I can't say."

"Well, give me some help."

"Pat, that's all I can tell you now." I got off the telephone.

Levering myself with the arms of a chair, I sank into its welcome depth.

The phone rang, and my wife informed me it was Pat Minarcin again. He had one more question, "Were there more hospitals involved than just Drake?" When I replied in the affirmative, the floodgates were open again. I explained to Pat the client-attorney relationship again and declared that I didn't know what I could or should do. Minarcin was understanding and got off the telephone.

The case haunted me. There had been some articles in the paper about Harvey, but nothing sensational. I knew that the whole story would eventually come out and that when it did, sensationalism would be a mild term for what followed. My wife and children had no idea what I was wrestling with. I needed to warn them of a possible public outcry and the potential for my being crucified in the media.

My wife, Diane, had many contacts in the community. My twenty-year-old son, Bill, was in school at the Cincinnati Art Academy, and my seventeen-year-old daughter, Kelly, was a senior at Seton High School. I was concerned about the consequences for them if I were included in the public castigation of my client. Young people can be cruel, and their friends might turn on them. The trauma might be unbearable.

At this point, only Harvey, Minarcin, and I were aware of the whole horrible story. I could go to the public defender's office and request to be removed as counsel. I would not have to reveal my reasons. I struggled with the problem for two days before deciding what to do. I had to offer my family the option of my removing myself from the case. I wanted the professional and personal challenge, but if my family was not willing to face it, I could abide by their decision.

The mood at dinner that night seemed light, with considerable bantering among us, but my stomach was churning. I was about to hand them a terrible burden, and they were completely unaware. I had intended to wait until after dinner to broach the subject, but I couldn't eat.

I laid down my knife and fork. They sensed the change and were silent.

"I have a case that is nothing like the ones I have told you about before. I have a client who is guilty of horrible crimes. When this comes to light, and it will, there is going to be a lot of publicity—most of it bad. The media will rip into my client, and probably me for defending him. You will get some of the fallout."

I saw concern on their faces, but no one said anything.

I continued, "I can ask to be relieved of the case. If you feel it will be too much stress for you, I will."

Kelly spoke first. "Did he do any of these crimes to little kids?"

"No."

"Then it won't bother me."

Bill shrugged. "I'm cool."

I looked to Diane.

"I trust your judgment. Do what you need to do."

My appetite returned, and I started to eat. They asked me a few innocuous questions about when this would break and whether I would be on TV, but the subject quickly slid away.

After dinner, I was still sitting in my chair, and Kelly came to my side. "Dad, are you going to be okay?"

I assured her that I would. I knew how much I was loved and trusted. I had the green light to go ahead.

In the following days the phone calls between Minarcin and me increased, sometimes to five or six a day. Minarcin told his secretary that any time I called, I was to be put through unless he was actually on the air.

I had resolved that Minarcin had to do the story, and that there were only two ways to go—sit on a bomb and hope that none of the sparks hit the fuse, or attempt to defuse the situation myself. There was no choice; I had to defuse the situation. Minarcin was my only manner of doing that. If I merely went to the authorities, they would have as much incredulity as I had when Minarcin first called.

In addition to the increased phone calls, I was meeting with Harvey every day, delving into the thinking and actions of one of the most prolific serial killers in the United States.

I began to feed some of the information to Minarcin. I now knew that arsenic and cyanide were two of the poisons Harvey used to take many of the lives.

During our conversations, we reached a pact. Minarcin would use none of the information I gave him without my specific agreement, unless he found a second source to confirm it. In that case he would inform me of his intention to use the material before putting it on the air.

Early in our discussions, I shared with Minarcin an item from Harvey's confession. Minarcin thought it incredible that when Jim Lawson took the statement from Donald Harvey and asked Harvey if he had killed any other people—a reasonable inquiry by a homicide detective—Lawson moved on to another subject when Harvey indicated that he didn't want to talk about it.

This was the portal to the entire matter. Harvey was talking, admitting a heinous crime, and now the investigator had opened the door, "Were there any other crimes?" and Harvey hesitated. If Lawson had pushed him, Harvey would almost certainly have admitted to other murders.

But Lawson had moved on and the door was closed.

I made a copy of the confession and turned it over to Minarcin. The reporter was in disbelief. One more question by Larson, and Minarcin's news story and my defense work for Harvey would have been for naught.

Why didn't he ask the question? We were perplexed. Was Lawson, an excellent homicide detective, just inattentive and not hear the answer? Did the police officer deliberately not go down that road to protect the city from lawsuits? Did they already know the answer? Was the detective just having a bad day?

It was not for many years that I had the opportunity to ask Lawson the question. Lawson explained his concern that Harvey's answers suggested he was laying the foundation for making a claim of mental incompetency. Lawson did not want to pursue the subject and have Harvey expound on his mental difficulties and perhaps ruin all the cases, including the John Powell case. A police interrogator must concentrate upon obtaining answers that will stand up in court. Lawson opted for staying with the issues at hand. The outcome would almost certainly have been different had the question been asked.

The information Minarcin was getting from his nurses was not enough to produce what he wanted, and he sought my assistance.

I was aghast when the newsman informed me that he intended for this to be a half-hour special solely on Harvey and the killings at Drake hospital. He had originally anticipated a thirty-second news story.

Broadcasting the story was an act of journalistic courage.

Minarcin convinced news director Cahalan and WCPO general manager Terry Connelly that he had the documentation to support the story. The decision to air the story was ultimately made by Donald L. Perris, president of Scripps-Howard Broadcasting, the station's parent. The company's attorneys, the law firm of Baker & Hostetler, reviewed the script and documentation before the broadcast.

On June 23, 1987, WCPO-TV presented a half-hour special report in the time slot normally reserved for the six o'clock newscast.

Minarcin avoided sensationalism in his manner of presentation, letting the story speak for itself. His dignified mien, with a touch of gray at his temples, was perfectly suited to the delivery of his message. He reviewed the account of the discovery that Powell's death was a homicide and Harvey's subsequent confession. He indicated that staff members had begun to raise questions as early as seven months earlier about the high incidence of deaths on Ward C-300 and suggested that as many as twenty-three were suspicious. He presented charts showing the numbers of deaths on each of five comparable wards during the period April 1986 to April 1987:

C-300 34
D-300 14
A-300 12
D-200 10
C-200   7

He added for comparison that the deaths on C-300 during the previous twelve-month period had been thirteen.

The program included interviews of hospital staff members with their identities disguised by blocking their features and altering their voices electronically. The staff members told of their suspicions of Harvey and of their unsuccessful attempts to induce their supervisors to take action. The steps taken to protect the anonymity of those who consented to be interviewed heightened the drama.

Minarcin also presented interviews with experts who said that when one hospital death caused by an unrelated staff member was uncovered, a vigorous investigation was imperative. One declared it was highly improbable that there were not more homicides to be discovered.

The station was meticulous in reporting that although Harvey had confessed to the murder of Powell and was in custody, he had not yet been convicted of any murder. Minarcin also stated three times that the station was not accusing Harvey of being a serial killer; they were just raising a question.

I was upset about one aspect of the show, but I couldn't really blame Pat Minarcin for it. I was sure his producer had been responsible for some of the background shots. They were eye-catching and dramatic, but I felt they were unfair to my client.

A clear, bright picture of John Powell as a healthy, happy extrovert was shown repeatedly. Several times the picture shifted to a dimly lit picture of Donald Harvey, shackled and disheveled, being led down a hall by a police officer.

I had agreed with Minarcin for him to broadcast the show, and I informed Harvey of the date and time of the broadcast. I felt overwhelmed by the situation. I had committed to a process that was out of control, and I couldn't predict the outcome. Harvey trusted me to do what was in his best interest. Had I violated that trust?

The broadcast lit a fuse of its own, and the fireworks exploded. The media jumped on it. The press was off and running.

The front-page article in the *Enquirer* the next day, headed "Review of Drake deaths urged," reported on the television program and added that the allegations would be discussed by the county commissioners in a closed-door meeting.

Various officials felt compelled to make statements. Radio and TV personalities were on the phone constantly seeking information from me.

I had chosen a partner for this dance and I would continue. My consistent answer to the press was, "No comment." During the broadcast, Minarcin had displayed the copy of Harvey's confession to Lawson. Questions from the police and prosecutors abounded immediately as they tried to find who had leaked that piece of internal information. The police assured the prosecutor they had not divulged it, and the prosecutor assured the police it did not come from his office.

From that day on, I was sure the police and the prosecutor suspected me of providing information to Minarcin.

I heard rumors that Hamilton County Prosecutor Art Ney's office was going to subpoena Pat Minarcin to appear before the grand jury in order to force him to reveal the sources of his information. I called Minarcin, and we arranged to meet for lunch. Minarcin told me that there was no possibility of his complying. Although Ohio law does not provide adequate immunity for reporters to protect their sources, he knew that he would be finished as an investigative reporter should he answer the prosecutor's questions. He was willing to serve a jail term if that were necessary.

Minarcin was, however, concerned that his wife be kept informed of what was happening if he were in jail. He didn't want her to panic from false information or lack of information. While I would have welcomed serving as the line of communication, we agreed that such an arrangement would be unwise and would heighten Art Ney's suspicion. In fact, Minarcin and I would need a go-between, also.

With Minarcin's agreement, I undertook to find an attorney who would represent Minarcin should the occasion arise and who would also serve as messenger. I thought of my friend Ray Faller, whose judgment I respected and whom I knew I could trust to keep anything I told him confidential. I went to Faller's home.

Falller's car was in his driveway, so I knew he was home. When Faller answered the doorbell, I said, "Let's take your dog for a walk in the park." Faller recognized my request for privacy and put his German shepherd on a leash.

After obtaining a promise of secrecy, I outlined the situation. Faller's first thoughts were of the ethics of the situation, primarily the client's rights. I assured him that Harvey knew what was happening and approved of my course of action. We then discussed the problems I had identified and others that Faller mentioned. Faller agreed to the role I proposed for him, should Ney proceed with the subpoena.

But Ney had other, more pressing concerns. The sources of Minarcin's information were much less important than the horror he implied. Minarcin had raised the question publicly: Was Powell's death an isolated murder, or did the police have a serial killer in custody?

PART II

A DEADLY LIFE

6. Growing Up Poor

Goldie Harvey was seventeen when her son, Donald, was born.
She was fourteen when she first met Ray Harvey in a smoky roadside tavern
outside Booneville, Kentucky. He immediately started putting a move on
her. Her teenage boyfriend was no match in competition with the good-
looking, assured Navy veteran. When she left the tavern that night, she was
with Ray.

Later, Goldie said of that meeting, "When I laid eyes on him, I said, 'Ray,
you be mine.' I thought he was the best-looking man. He had the prettiest
mouthful of teeth."

The difference in their ages was a plus to Goldie. She wasn't really looking for a husband; she was looking for a father. She had a stepfather, but that
wasn't the same as having someone of her own. She was eager to leave home.

Goldie had a difficult childhood. She was raped, beaten, and left for dead
when she was twelve years old. To get help, she crawled nearly a mile from
the hollow where she had been attacked. Her parents were so certain she was
dying that they didn't take her to a doctor for two weeks. Her head injury
severely affected her memory, and she never recovered full use of her right
arm. In that rural community, rape was considered a disgrace for the victim
and her family. Goldie's mother concealed the rape by telling everyone that
Goldie had polio. Goldie dropped out of school.

Ray wasn't looking for a daughter, but Goldie's pretty, unsophisticated,
little-girl look captured his fancy. Their courtship was rapid. They were mar-

ried just a few weeks later. When Goldie and Ray were married, Goldie was fifteen and Ray was thirty-one.

Ray owned a three-room farmhouse on Island Creek in Booneville, Kentucky, near Goldie's parents. Goldie loved the countryside, beautiful with green, rolling hills, a pretty little creek, and plenty of trees. But it was poor country. Although there were seams of coal near the surface, the veins were not rich enough for serious mining. Small-scale tobacco farming was the main source of income. Ray's eighteen acres of creek bottom and steep hillside barely provided a living.

After two years in Booneville, Ray decided they needed to migrate to Ohio so he could get a job in a factory. Goldie was pregnant. He got a job as a door-fitter with Mosler Safe Company in Hamilton, Ohio.

Donald was born in Mercy Hospital in Hamilton on April 15, 1952. He weighed eight pounds, fourteen ounces and was twenty-one inches long. Goldie had gained a lot of weight satisfying her craving for pork chops and strawberries. She named him Donald after a character in a favorite radio soap opera.

Donald's first six months were difficult for him and his parents. He was colicky and, according to Goldie, he screamed all day and all night. The parents took shifts in caring for him. She would try to comfort him until midnight, when his father would come home from work and take over. One night he fell asleep holding the baby, and Donald fell to the floor. Although Donald didn't seem to be seriously injured, his soft spot hadn't closed.

In spite of the problems, Goldie was proud of her baby and loved to show him to family and friends—a living doll. But she was unprepared to be a mother. Years later, Donald told an interviewer, "A child should not have been raising a child."

Donald had chronic ear infections. When he was about two years old, he was admitted to Mercy Hospital with pneumonia and a fever of 104 degrees. Because of the fever, he was having seizures.

While Goldie was preoccupied with her baby, she began to suspect that Ray was not being faithful. One night he came home "smelling different," and she knew he had been with another woman. Goldie and Ray had what Goldie called "good rug-see" fights. She said that meant, "He'd knock me down so I'd see the rug, then I'd knock him down so he'd see the rug."

One time Goldie had to go to the dentist for repair of her teeth after a fight. Another time, the police intervened when she threw a bottle through the windshield of Ray's car.

When Donald was three, she left Ray and returned to Owsley County in eastern Kentucky, where she moved in with her parents. Ray followed three weeks later. They moved back into their house, but Ray was home only about two weekends a month. Donald later described the situation as "separated, but sharing a house."

The house had white siding and a tin roof. It was primitive, with no running water and a wood stove for cooking and a coal stove for heat. Even as a small child, Donald had the chore of drawing water from the well and bringing it into the house. He remembers drawing water when he was not heavy enough to counterbalance a full bucket. Going outside to the toilet was inconvenient at best and often uncomfortable, especially in cold weather.

In the winter, they closed off one room of the three-room house to conserve heat. Donald was also responsible for bringing in coal for the stove.

The family had very little money. They lived on what they could grow in a small garden. Entertainment was primarily attending funerals and church revivals. Donald remembers "all-day preaching and dinner on the grounds" held in graveyards.

When Donald was five years old, Ray took him to observe the backwaters of a big flood. Donald was riding on the running board of the truck and fell off. He didn't lose consciousness, but his eyes rolled together. He had a cut ten to twelve centimeters long on the back of his head.

Donald said he had a lot of earaches, which he attributed to the injury, but they may have been the result of the earlier infection. According to Katherine Ramsland, Ph.D. and author of *The Criminal Mind*, (Writer's Digest Books), some neurological studies indicate that many serial killers have experienced some kind of brain injury. She wrote that there is no evidence that the injury causes one to be a killer, but suggested that neural processes might be damaged in a way that diminished inhibitions.

Donald had what he called a "treehouse," but it was actually in the loft of an old tobacco barn. He kept his treasures there: candy, pennies, a belt with two cap guns, and a cap rifle. He had no pets.

The proximity of the extended family was both a blessing and a curse. They were often in and out of each other's homes. On the weekends that Ray was home, Goldie sent Donald to stay with her mother. Donald and Granny loved each other, and Donald was happy when he visited her. But Donald had an uncle—Goldie's half brother, Wayne Byrd—nine years older, who started sexually abusing him when Donald was four. The relationship continued for sixteen years, even after Wayne was married. Donald said they had at least four hundred sexual encounters during that time.

Wayne used Donald primarily as an aid to masturbation, but they also engaged in oral sex. The relationship was suspended when Granny caught them together in bed. Donald was about fourteen. Granny gave Donald a lecture. He doesn't know what she did about Wayne, but she never allowed them to sleep in the same bed again.

Donald is ambivalent about his feelings for Wayne, for Wayne was good to him in many ways, giving him affection that he felt he did not get at home. Wayne treated him well, taking him to movies and giving him candy.

A much older neighbor, Dan Thomas, also sexually abused Donald for fifteen years, beginning when he was about five. Donald didn't like him, but Thomas gave him money. Donald would sometimes refuse to go outside and play because he was "afraid of the old man in the cornfield." He tried to break off the relationship, but Thomas threatened to harm his mother if he did.

According to Donald, his sexual relationships with Wayne and Dan Thomas were initially rape. He began to enjoy the sexual activity, and by the time he was about ten years old he was often the initiator.

As a child, Donald always wanted to be the center of attention. When his position was threatened by the birth of his sister, Pat, Donald reacted by becoming "mother's little helper," although he was only five years old. He took up feminine pursuits in the home, and when his brother, Tony, was born two years later Donald was cooking and cleaning. By the time he was ten, Goldie would leave Pat and Tony in his care. He craved, and received, attention and approval from the women in his family. The men reacted negatively. His father was practically a stranger to him, and his grandfather derided him, calling him "Polly Ann."

When Donald was nine, a woman neighbor gave him a baby chick as a pet. His mother told him angrily that he couldn't keep it. He hid the chick in the barn for several days, but his mother found it and ordered him to get rid of it. He reacted by taking the chick into the yard and hacking it in two with a hoe. Relating the incident years later, he said that he found an odd release from anger, tension, and frustration. He felt powerful.

Donald's first experience in nursing came when he was about fourteen. Granny was ill and confined to her bed. He did her washing and ironing and helped clean her house. He took care of her, bathing her and treating the sores that developed on her back.

Neat almost to the point of being fastidious, Donald always wanted to wear dress clothes to school. He and his mother argued about his clothes. He refused to wear jeans and wanted his clothes pressed. He always wanted his hair cut neatly.

The girls liked him. He thinks the boys just hadn't started to like girls yet, and so they called him a sissy for hanging out with the girls; but they didn't pick on him or start fights. He was not good at contact sports although he was good at volleyball.

He was intelligent and a good student, but he had to leave school when he was in the ninth grade. He was sawing a piece of wood in a shop class and cut it too short. His teacher told him that he would have to either stay after school and work or pay $3.20 for the wood. He couldn't stay late because he lived eleven miles from the school and would miss his bus. His father said he couldn't pay for the wood. At that time, Ray had hurt his back and was unable to work. Donald said he was not allowed to continue in school unless he paid the fee.

He moved in with neighbors, Finley Bowles and his wife, Lizzie. Finley Bowles was ill and had a wooden leg. Donald received room and board and forty dollars a month for helping with housekeeping and providing his nursing care. He gave him bed baths and changed his clothes and his linens. He took his blood pressure and temperature. Lizzie Bowles was diabetic, and Donald gave her insulin injections.

Donald used the money to enroll in The American School, a correspondence school in Chicago. He received a diploma from the school in April 1968, and obtained his G.E.D. that same year. The *Booneville People's Journal* printed a story about his graduation, complete with a picture of him. The article stated, in part, "Donald Ray Harvey, Box 171, Booneville, was graduated from The American School, Chicago, Illinois, and awarded a diploma completing high school. . . . Donald completed all high school courses in one year, four months, and nine days." He told the reporter he planned a career as a male nurse and hoped to enter a nursing school in the near future.

Donald moved to Cincinnati when he was sixteen and lived with Wayne and his second wife, Carol, for a year and a half. After a couple of temporary jobs, he obtained employment with Micro Mechanical Finishing Company through Wayne's influence.

During this period, he had his first sexual encounters in which he was an equal partner. His partners were Gene, who was a teacher, and Jim, a coworker at Micro. He doesn't remember their last names.

One snowy night Donald walked to a convenience store for a can of pop. He noticed a slightly built man with thin graying hair seated in a van in the parking lot. The man called Donald over and started a conversation. Donald recognized him as the owner of a produce shop he often passed. He learned that he was James "Little Jimmy" Peluso, brother of the mayor of Newport.

Donald thought Peluso had been watching for him. He figured that Peluso recognized his homosexuality by the way he walked, because after a few minutes, Peluso said, "I want to blow you."

Donald replied, "Why not?" and climbed into the van.

That was all Peluso asked then. He didn't ask Donald to reciprocate. He took Donald's telephone number and called him a few days later to arrange to pick him up. They began a relationship that lasted off and on for fifteen years. They engaged in sex in the van in rest areas and sometimes a motel. Their sex roles were interchangeable. Donald described himself as "an old man's darling." Peluso paid for everything and gave Donald money.

While working at Micro, Donald fell through a catwalk and tore a ligament in his foot. He couldn't work, but Wayne refused to put in an accident report. Donald returned to his parents' home in Kentucky.

In 1970, at the age of eighteen, Donald left home again and moved to London, Kentucky.

7. An Orderly Progression

What launched Donald on a hospital career? Was it chance, fate, or fulfilling his ambition to be a nurse? A case could be made for any of the three. Certainly his experience in caring for Mr. and Mrs. Bowles was a significant factor.

Donald was not looking for a job when he went to Marymount Hospital in London, Laurel County, Kentucky. He was there to visit his step-grandfather, Elbert Byrd, who was recovering from pneumonia. At the hospital he met two orderlies, Randy White and Millard Patton. They told him there was a job opening for another orderly.

Donald applied for the job. Marymount was a small Catholic hospital run by the Sisters of Charity. The interviewers were impressed by his good looks, his polite manner, and his knowledge of procedures in caring for the sick. His lack of formal credentials may have even been a plus, because he couldn't command a high rate of pay. They hired him immediately.

A week later, Millard helped him move from Booneville. They started a sexual relationship in Millard's car on the way back to London. Donald moved in with Millard and his mother temporarily, sharing a room with Millard. Millard's father was in a tuberculosis sanatorium.

Millard's mother was pleasant to Donald, but she didn't want him living there. The room had two beds, so Donald doesn't think Millard's mother was aware of their sexual relationship. After three days, Harvey rented a room from Randy's mother, Helen June White, his second cousin, who was employed in the office at the hospital.

Randy was a transsexual entertainer—a drag queen who worked as a female impersonator at a nightclub in Lexington on weekends. He lived at home. After Donald's first day at work, Randy invited him to have a drink in his room. They had a couple of drinks and listened to music.

When Randy made some disparaging remarks about Millard, Donald realized that he was starting to hit on him. He went along at first, but Randy wanted anal sex, and Donald objected. Donald later claimed that Randy raped him. He was sick and off from work for two days.

The hospital had no organized training program for new employees, and Donald had to learn on the job. At first he accompanied Millard and learned from watching him. His supervisor, Margaret Rudd, was a highly intelligent nurse who gave him a lot of instruction, but only at the time that a need arose. Donald said that although he was shown how to insert a catheter, a patient actually taught him how to perform the procedure.

Randy quit his job at the hospital three days after Harvey started to work, and Millard left after about two weeks. Donald was the only male orderly for a year.

The sisters refused to catheterize male patients, so Donald was called in on his days off and even in the middle of the night for that procedure. As a favor to the sisters, a police car would come pick him up, wait for him at the hospital, and return him home afterward. Donald liked that extra duty. It made him feel important, and he would receive a half day's pay for one hour of work.

Donald had started work at Marymount on May 11, 1970. He had just turned eighteen. On May 30 he was working on the night shift. On duty in the ward that night were a charge nurse, two licensed practical nurses (LPNs), and another aide. Donald was responsible for the care of nine patients. He measured and recorded their temperatures, blood pressures, and volumes of urine, and provided general nursing care. He had no preps for surgery that night, because it was a weekend.

Logan D. Evans, an eighty-eight-year-old man in room 217, was particularly troublesome. Evans was an alcoholic who had suffered a stroke and was partially paralyzed and semi-conscious. His family had abandoned him. Donald had already cleaned him up several times that night. The nurse sent Donald in to care for him again about 10:00 P.M. Evans was covered with feces and his catheter had come out, wetting the bed.

Evans reached out for Donald with his one good arm, clutching at his clothes. His hand was covered with feces, which he smeared over Donald. Harvey lost his temper. He put a sheet of blue plastic over Evans's face and smothered him with a pillow. He listened to his heart with a stethoscope. Satisfied that there was no heartbeat, Harvey disposed of the plastic and cleaned Evans up one more time, dressing him in a clean hospital gown. He changed the bed and fluffed the pillows.

Then he notified the nurse on duty that he thought Evans was dead. He had no fear of getting caught. He knew there would be no autopsy, because the autopsy rate there was almost nil. Evans had been expected to die.

More than eighteen years later, an interviewer asked Harvey, "How did you feel after killing a man?"

Harvey replied, "Relieved. When I killed Logan Evans, I was killing Dan Thomas, Millard, and Randy White . . . and Donnie. The old Donnie Harvey that people did things to was dead. The new Donald Harvey was in charge."

The next death Harvey caused was an accident, the result of Harvey's youth and inexperience and a nurse's error. The day after Harvey killed Logan Evans, a nurse directed him to catheterize James Tyree. Tyree, a sixty-nine-year-old white man, was hospitalized for lung and bowel problems. He was conscious and objected, saying that he did not need a catheter. He was correct; the nurse had made an error in transcribing the doctor's instructions and had written the order for the wrong patient. Harvey, however, tried to force the procedure on the patient, because he didn't want the nurse to think he couldn't do his job.

Tyree let him proceed, but then winced in pain and yelled, "No! Take it out! Take it out!" He rose up in bed, and Harvey pushed him back down. He struggled up again, and Harvey pushed him harder, using the heel of his hand because he didn't want to contaminate his rubber gloves. Tyree vomited blood and died. Harvey screamed for the nurse. She sent him home to change his clothes because they had been spattered with blood.

He changed and returned to work. The hospital reimbursed him for his gray suede shoes, which he had been unable to clean. Nothing else was ever said to him at the hospital about Tyree's death, except one of the sisters told him, "Don't worry about it. It was an accident. Patients die. It happens to all of us. You must never speak of this matter to anyone."

Elizabeth Wyatt, forty-two, was slowly dying of lung cancer. On Monday morning, June 22, 1970, she had been in the hospital for two weeks. She was very thin. Donald had become well acquainted with her, since he fed her most of her meals. He talked with her often because they knew a lot of people in common, and they found that they were distant relatives by marriage. He remembers that she wore her dark hair, with just a touch of white, pulled back. She had long, pretty fingernails.

He was aware that she had been praying to die. After her family visited her that day, she told Harvey, "I wish I could just close my eyes and go to sleep, because I'm happy. I don't want to die in front of my children or my husband."

With his newfound power to be in control, he decided to honor her request. She was in an oxygen tent, and he turned her supply of oxygen extremely low. He said, "Good night," and left the room. Four hours later a nurse found her dead.

To Harvey, the death of Eugene McQueen was closely related to that of Elizabeth Wyatt, even though his methods were quite different. McQueen, forty-three, was also in terminal condition, and Harvey considers that he hastened his death as an act of mercy. McQueen suffered from cerebral palsy and lung congestion. Harvey, in the process of cleaning him up and changing his bed, turned him over on his face, which he knew not to do.

McQueen died rapidly from drowning in his own fluid, i.e., the congestion in his lungs. Harvey went out and told the nurse that McQueen looked bad, but she told him to remove his IV and go ahead with his care.

Harvey turned him back over to a supine position and completed his bath. Harvey changed the linen on the other bed in that room and then told that patient's visitor, who had been waiting in the hall, that she could come back in. She looked at McQueen and commented on how ill he looked. Harvey said, "He's been like that all day."

McQueen lay there for over four hours before Dr. Adams discovered him dead when making his rounds. The nursing supervisor should have made rounds every two hours, but had failed to do so. The hospital called his death an accident and covered up the details. As long as Harvey worked at the hospital, the nurses and Dr. Adams kidded him about having cleaned up a dead man without knowing that he was dead.

Harve Williams's death two days later was an accident. Williams, seventy-two, diabetic and blind, complained of chest pains, probably the beginning of a heart attack, and Donald was told to give him oxygen. Harvey brought an oxygen tank to the room and hooked him up. The valve assembly on the tank was faulty and gave a false reading. The gauge indicated that the tank was almost full when it was actually empty. Without the oxygen,

Williams went into cardiac arrest and died.

A sister angrily accused Harvey of killing the man because of his ineptitude. She apologized the next day. Sister Agnes Martha instructed Harvey to tell no one about the use of a faulty valve, because the hospital could be sued. Harvey labeled the faulty valve for repair and returned it to the shelf in the storage room. During the time that Harvey was at Marymount, the valve was never repaired, and it figured in other deaths that were not accidental.

Harvey and Ben H. Gilbert were adversaries. Gilbert's antagonism initially stemmed from two accidents. Gilbert, eighty-one, was temporarily in a bed in the hall. Harvey tripped over Gilbert's drainage tube and pulled the catheter out of his penis. Later, when Gilbert was in a room, Harvey, cleaning up the room, broke a light bulb in a wall socket. Gilbert called Harvey, "A demon from hell."

Harvey's hatred of Gilbert was precipitated by aggression on Gilbert's part. Gilbert waited just inside the door to his room, and when Harvey came in knocked him unconscious with a urinal and poured its contents over him. Harvey was taken to the emergency room on a stretcher. Gilbert claimed he thought Harvey was a burglar. Years later, during a deposition, Harvey conceded that Gilbert, mentally confused and in a strange place, might well have acted out of fear, not malice.

Harvey's opportunity to retaliate came the next day, when he had to catheterize Gilbert again. He tied Gilbert down and placed a burn cradle over him so that if anyone came into the room they could not tell what he was doing. He inserted an oversized catheter, a #20 intended for female patients instead of a standard #18. Then he straightened out a coat hanger and shoved the wire through the catheter about two feet, puncturing Gilbert's bladder and bowel. Gilbert went into instant shock, breaking into a cold sweat and going into a coma. Harvey disposed of the wire and replaced the #20 catheter with a #18. Gilbert died of peritonitis four days later.

While admitting his own guilt, Donald also faults the hospital management for failing to prevent him from being alone with Gilbert. He said, "I should never have been allowed to take care of him again as a patient. The charge nurse knew what had happened to me the night before, but assigned him to my patient load anyway."

Harvey said that killing Gilbert was a turning point for him. Although he had caused deaths through accident, ineptitude, anger, and what he considered compassion, none had been planned. Gilbert's death was premeditated.

8. Strange Encounters

Donald met Vernon Midden at Marymount Hospital under appropriately bizarre circumstances involving a body part.

Vernon, an undertaker in London, Kentucky, came to the hospital to pick up an amputated leg, because the patient's family wanted it embalmed and buried. Donald carried the leg to the hearse.

Vernon, however, had a secondary agenda. He had been wanting to meet Donald, because Randy and Millard had told him that Donald could be gay. Although Vernon was married and had three children, he was interested in Donald sexually.

Donald was favorably impressed with Vernon at sight. Vernon was a good-looking man, well built, with neat brown hair. His attire, which Donald later described as "like a preacher," appealed to Donald's own taste in dress.

Vernon immediately showed Donald that he thought of him as a person, not just an underling at the hospital. He made a dinner date with him. That evening he met Donald at the hospital when he got off work and took him to the Country Kitchen restaurant. After dinner, they had a sexual encounter in Vernon's car, beginning a relationship that lasted for seven months.

Donald was eighteen and Vernon thirty-six. According to Donald, when a gay couple establishes a stable relationship (as opposed to casual sexual encounters), there is almost always a significant difference in their ages. He, at least, always preferred older men.

During the time that Vernon and Donald were lovers, Vernon often came to see Donald at Helen June's house. Donald was amused that gossips started to talk about that, assuming that Vernon was having an affair with Helen June.

They also met at the funeral home. Vernon's sexual interests went beyond heterosexual and homosexual encounters with the living. Donald said Vernon abused corpses. One of his favorite stunts was to embalm male corpses with an artificially induced erection.

Donald said that Vernon also liked to persuade young men to allow him to have oral sex with them when they were lying in a casket. He wanted to simulate a sex act with a corpse by having them be cold, such as by sitting in a tub of cold water before getting in the casket.

Donald refused to climb into a casket.

Donald spent much time in the embalming room with Vernon while he was working. Vernon showed him a lot about his work. He showed him embalming techniques and makeup. He would pay Donald fifteen or twenty dollars to help him clean and dress a corpse.

He taught Donald how different causes of death could be detected. For example, he showed him how smothering changes the appearance of the body, including the presence of small fibers if the victim has been smothered with a fabric, such as a pillow. He pointed out the tiny hemorrhages called petechiae that are always present in tissues such as eyelids when a victim has been smothered, even though there might be no obvious external indications of trauma. Donald also remembers Vernon's description of the appearance of a body of a person who died from poisoning by carbon monoxide. Donald was interested then out of curiosity. Later he put this education to practical use.

Vernon practiced witchcraft and introduced Donald to the occult. He hosted meetings of a coven that he said was about sixty years old. Vernon didn't allow Donald to take part in the rituals, or even to observe the most secret practices, because Donald had not been initiated. Donald, however, knew that Vernon appropriated some organs, livers and testicles, for use in the occult rituals.

Donald did attend some of the meetings of the coven. Margaret Rudd, the RN who was his supervisor at Marymount, was a member of the coven. At meetings, she served a tea. Donald pretended to drink it, but did not swallow because he was sure it contained drugs. Donald says he drank alcoholic beverages, sometimes to excess, but he never took drugs.

Margaret Rudd abused both drugs and alcohol. Donald said she frequently came to work unfit to discharge her duties. One of her coping mechanisms was to overdose patients with morphine so that they would sleep through her shift. Control of drug inventories was very lax at the hospital at that time, and the discrepancies between prescribed dosages and actual usage were undetected. Sometimes Margaret would appropriate for herself drugs that had been prescribed for a patient and would give the patient an injection of sterile water.

Margaret and Donald became friends, although there was never any sexual interest between them. She was a friendly, outgoing person, who took him under her wing.

Donald says that almost all homosexual men have at least one female friend. Donald used the term "fag hag," meaning a woman who likes homosexual men. She knew that he was homosexual, although he had not yet come out of the closet. She urged Donald to have therapy to resolve what she called his "ambiguity."

Margaret was interested in men. She told Donald to let her know whenever any male patient had particularly large sexual organs. She would manufacture an excuse to look. For example, she would instruct Donald to spill water on the bed, and then she would come in to help him change the bed, or she would "check to see that he had inserted a catheter correctly."

Donald himself had no interest in patients from a sexual standpoint and vehemently objected to an implication that he did. Whenever he was wrongly accused of anything, Donald really felt strongly about defending himself. This theme recurs repeatedly in his history.

Years later, an interviewer asked Donald, "Why have you strongly denied some accusations while readily admitting more serious charges?"

Donald replied, "When I am guilty of it, I'll admit to it. I ain't going to admit to something I didn't do."

As his attorney, I don't believe the last part of that statement. But that comes much later.

9. A Pattern of Destruction

Donald Harvey had been responsible for six deaths at Marymount Hospital during his first three months as an orderly. Two of the deaths were accidents, but one was voluntary manslaughter and three were murders. But Harvey didn't use that word. He preferred to think that he had caused deaths, induced deaths, or even "taken care of" patients. The hospital staff didn't question the deaths, although the sisters told Harvey not to talk about them.

Not talking about patients was the established norm at the hospital. Harvey had been told that it was because of patient confidentiality. In a March 1993 deposition for the Laurel County Circuit Court, Harvey said that a baby so deformed that it was referred to as "the egg" was born there and sent to a special hospital in Louisville, and Harvey was specifically told to mention it to nobody. He thinks the family was told the baby was born dead. He said he was also cautioned to say nothing about a six-month-old baby who died of pneumonia. He believes that Margaret Rudd caused the baby's death by an error of either omission or commission. Although he had no contact with either of these cases, the policy of secrecy had a strong influence upon him. Harvey felt that he could kill with impunity.

Maude Nichols, sixty-four years old, lay in bed screaming with pain. She had been moved to Marymount from an unlicensed nursing home. She had bedsores so bad that her bones showed, and maggots were crawling in the sores. No one wanted to give her care. Harvey went to the storage room and got the faulty oxygen valve, which was still there awaiting repair. He exchanged it for the valve on the oxygen tank in her room. She died at 4:45 A.M. on August 15, 1970. Harvey returned the faulty valve to the storage room.

Two weeks later, William Bowling, fifty-eight, was brought to the hospital as an emergency, because he was having difficulty breathing. Harvey put him in a wheelchair and rolled him to the emergency room, where he put him on an operating table and called for a doctor. Ollie Gaines, the nurse on duty, tried unsuccessfully to reach either Dr. Smith, who was on call, or Dr. Adams, his backup. She left a call for Dr. Adams and instructed Harvey to put an oxygen cannula on Bowling. Then she rushed to take care of another emergency. Harvey put the cannula on Bowling, but he did not turn on the flow. His inaction was intentional, but spontaneous. He wanted to end the patient's struggles to breathe.

Bowling died of a massive heart attack. Harvey informed the nurse, and she removed the cannula while checking Bowling for vital signs. He lay in the emergency room for over five hours before Dr. Adams came and pronounced him dead. Dr. Adams questioned Harvey about the removal of the cannula, but was satisfied with the explanation that nurse Gaines had removed it after Bowling was dead. He did not ask whether the oxygen flow had been turned on.

The faulty oxygen valve served Harvey again. Viola Reed Wyan, sixty-three, was suffering from leukemia and electrolyte imbalance and was unconscious. Harvey said she smelled really bad. She had blood in her stools. He decided that the time had come for her to die. He arranged the curtains around her bed to give him privacy and placed a wastebasket behind the partially closed door so that he would hear if anyone started to enter the room. Avoiding the use of a pillow, because of what he had learned from Vernon, he laid a small plastic bag over her face.

As he was tucking the plastic into place, he heard a noise. By the time a nurse had entered and pulled back the curtain, the plastic bag was out of sight. He said, "I'm just finishing up," tugged at the corner of the sheet, and left the room. Later he returned with the faulty oxygen valve and exchanged it for the one in use. He was not present when Viola Wyan died, but it was his job to remove the oxygen equipment from the room. He replaced the tag on the bad valve and returned it to the storage room.

Margaret E. Harrison was ninety-one years old, hospitalized following a heart attack. She was fed with a baby bottle, a sight upsetting to Harvey. He was saddened to see this return to infant behavior. He gave her an overdose of morphine, Demerol, and codeine intended for another patient. He monitored her heartbeat with a stethoscope until her pulse rate dropped to zero and she stopped breathing.

In January 1971 Donald's relationship with Vernon started to go sour, and Donald was depressed. Vernon liked a forceful form of sex that was unpleasant to Donald. Donald started wanting to get away from Marymount and from Vernon. He had fantasies of embalming Vernon alive. Donald said later that depression was the reason he killed four patients at Marymount Hospital that month.

Donald's memory of that period is hazy, partly because of the passage of time and partly because of his emotional state then. Records show that Sam Carroll died on January 9, Maggie Rawlins on January 15, Silas Butner on January 23, and John V. Combs on January 26. Donald is sure he was responsible for all four deaths, although he was not convicted of killing Carroll.

The relationship between Donald's depression and these deaths is complex, but Donald apparently projected his feelings onto the patients. He saw their situations as hopeless and concluded that they wanted to die. By ending their suffering, he eased his own.

He felt sorry for Sam Carroll, an eighty-year-old man with pneumonia and an obstruction of his small intestine. Carroll had one oversized testicle; the other had been removed. Harvey felt that Carroll was suffering too much and decided to put an end to it. Although Carroll could talk, Harvey did not discuss that decision with him. He again took the faulty oxygen valve from the storage room and replaced the valve that was in use. Deprived of oxygen, Carroll died.

Maggie Rawlins was hospitalized for treatment of a bad burn on her arm, caused by falling on an open grate, apparently while intoxicated. Harvey smothered her with a pillow, but he put a plastic bag between her face and the pillow in order to avoid any fibers in her airways. Mrs. Rawlins's son operated a funeral home, and although Harvey expected no autopsy, Vernon's information had made him more cautious about the possibility of detection.

Harvey thought that Silas Butner, a sixty-two-year-old man with kidney problems, was not being properly cared for by the women on the staff of the hospital because he was African-American. He tried to smother Butner several times, but was interrupted each time. He fell back on his old familiar process and used the faulty oxygen valve. He became concerned that his role in Butner's death might be discovered, because there was an autopsy, but the true cause of death was not detected.

Harvey considered John Combs, sixty-eight, who had a bad heart and difficulty in breathing, to be a "nice man in distress." Combs was in a private room. Harvey tried to smother him with a plastic bag, using a stethoscope to monitor his heartbeat, but he was unsuccessful. Once more, he used the faulty oxygen valve as his instrument of death. He described Combs's death as a mercy killing.

Almost two months elapsed before Harvey killed again. His final victim at Marymount was Milton Bryant Sasser, a ninety-year-old man with congestive heart failure. Harvey gave him an overdose of morphine stolen from the medicine cabinet at the nurses' station. He made the mistake of trying to dispose of the hypodermic needle in a toilet, stopping it up. The maintenance man at the hospital discovered the needle; however, no one recognized a connection between the hypodermic needle and Sasser's death.

Donald's personal problems, unconnected with Marymount, erupted at this time.

His life was falling apart. He was breaking up with Vernon, he was depressed, and he was drinking heavily. He set a fire in the bathroom of an empty apartment in the building where he shared an apartment with Helen June, apparently in an unsuccessful suicide attempt, hoping to die of asphyxiation. The damage was minimal, but he was arrested for arson. He paid a fifty-dollar fine.

A neighbor in that same building gave him some of her husband's clothing, without her husband's knowledge. The man saw him wearing the clothes and called the police, claiming that Donald had stolen the items.

Donald had gone to Frankfort, Kentucky, to apply for a job in the state forestry service. He visited a family named Hodges. He and the Hodges's daughter, Ruth Ann, got drunk together. Although Donald had experienced many homosexual encounters, he had never come out of the closet and was confused about his sexuality. When they were drunk, Ruth Ann boasted that she had never met a man she couldn't bed.

Donald remembers very little of the episode. He said he remembers being naked in bed with her but does not recall sexual intercourse. However, nine months later Ruth Ann Hodges gave birth to a son and named Donald as the father. The baby was given up for adoption. In his deposition for the Laurel County Circuit Court years later, Donald declared that he had two sons, but he refused to name the mother of the other. On another occasion, he denied that he ever had any children, although he said he had heterosexual intercourse twice. (See chapter 10.)

That night in Frankfort, the Hodgeses called the police, and Donald was taken to the police station. He awoke the next morning with no memory of the previous night. When interrogated, he told the police that he had been responsible for fifteen deaths at Marymount Hospital. He was not believed. The police had a warrant for his arrest on suspicion of the burglary in his apartment building, so he was returned to London to face that charge.

The police were not particularly interested in pursuing the case of suspected burglary. They were interested in learning about the coven. The sheriff offered Donald a deal; he would drop the charges if Donald would tell him about the group practicing witchcraft. Donald, already breaking up with Vernon, was willing to tell what he knew.

He repeated his confession that he had been responsible for fifteen deaths at Marymount Hospital. Again, he was not believed, and he was advised to see a psychiatrist.

Donald did not return to Marymount Hospital. He sent in his resignation by Helen June White, and she brought him his final paycheck. His last day at work had been March 27.

Donald went to a psychiatrist at the Cumberland River Comprehensive Care Center in London. He saw a psychiatrist three times but did not continue the therapy. He returned to Owsley County.

On June 16, 1971, he enlisted in the U.S. Air Force.

10. Searching for Direction

Donald's life was in disarray. He had been arrested and was unsure that his troubles with the police were over. He had betrayed his friends by talking to the police about occult practices. He had broken up with his lovers. He had resigned from his job to avoid being fired for his conduct off the job. He was getting drunk and losing control. He had even made an unsuccessful attempt at suicide.

Enlisting in the Air Force was an attempt to escape from his problems. Joining the military service would take him away from Kentucky.

At first, it worked. Donald was sent to Lackland Air Force Base in San Antonio, Texas. He enjoyed basic training. He experienced discipline for the first time in his life.

Still searching for a spiritual foundation, he joined the Church of Jesus Christ of Latter-Day Saints in San Antonio. He quickly found that to be a mistake for him. He was unable to abide by the strict rules of conduct.

Upon completion of his basic training, he was assigned to Travis Air Force Base in San Francisco. He worked as an administrative clerk in the Civil Engineering Squadron Orderly Room, keeping regular office hours, 8:00 A.M.–5:00 P.M. His duties included picking up the mail and distributing it. While working there, he intercepted a letter to his commanding officer from the FBI, inquiring about his time in London, Kentucky. He destroyed the letter and never heard anything more about it.

He lived on the base. He had one homosexual encounter at the base with

Jim, a veteran who came to his room. Donald said he had an urge to kill Jim, but he refrained because he had no way to dispose of the body. It is significant that the deterrent was fear of getting caught, not an aversion to killing.

In San Francisco, Donald pursued his interest in the occult. He checked out books on witchcraft from the library. He visited a Satanic church, although he didn't join and participated in no rituals.

His escape from his past was temporary. He became depressed again and took an overdose of NyQuil. Follow-up of that incident led to disclosure of his previous arrest and subsequent therapy. Because he had concealed that history from the recruiter, he was discharged from the Air Force on March 9, 1972, after nine months of service. His discharge was classified as medical, under honorable conditions.

Donald returned to the Midwest. He lived briefly with Wayne in Cincinnati while looking unsuccessfully for a job. Wayne wanted to resume their homosexual affair, but Donald refused. He now felt that such a relationship was improper because they were in the same family.

He went home to Booneville for the weekend, and after breakfast got into an argument with his family. They were critical of him for leaving the military and for his homosexuality. Donald was depressed about the argument and about his difficulty in finding a job. He went to his room and took an overdose of Placydil and Equanil. After a short time, his father knocked on his door. Receiving no response, he entered and found Donald unconscious. Unable to revive him, his family called the life squad.

Donald was taken first to an emergency hospital in Irvine, where they pumped out his stomach. Then they transferred him to the VA hospital in Lexington. He was a patient in the hospital for three months and an outpatient for a year and a half, receiving psychiatric care. While he was an outpatient, he worked in medical records as a volunteer.

When Donald was discharged from the VA hospital as an inpatient, his parents told him he was no longer welcome at home. He lived at the YMCA. He saw an advertisement for an orderly at Cardinal Hill Convalescent Hospital in Lexington. He applied and was hired. He worked at Cardinal Hill for five months full time and another two years part time. His career there was uneventful.

He also worked six months for Good Samaritan Hospital in Lexington as a ward clerk and for General Telephone for a year as a switchboard operator.

At the VA hospital, Donald met a social worker, Dave, with whom he participated in a suicide support group. Donald said that Dave was active in

Satanism, but this time he didn't get involved. Instead, he joined a Roman Catholic church. He attended mass every morning and seriously considered becoming a lay brother.

Donald felt the need for a higher power in his life, but he lacked the self-discipline to follow through on any commitment.

His plans to become a lay brother were aborted and Donald left the church when he met Russell Addison, a psychiatric patient at Good Samaritan. Russell had been picked up for homosexual solicitation. Donald and Russell started a relationship and lived together for ten months, the first time Donald had ever lived with a lover. They had an open relationship; i.e., Russell dated both men and women, mostly men, and Donald played around with other men.

While Donald was living with Russell, he went to a gay bar called The Living Room, located on Main Street in downtown Lexington. There he met Ken Estes, and they became lovers. They moved to Cincinnati, where they lived together intermittently for five years.

Donald got a job at St. Luke Hospital in Fort Thomas, Kentucky, as a ward clerk. He worked there for six months.

Donald and Ken bought a house together next to St. Ann School in Covington, Kentucky. They lived there for a year. They sold the house and split up, but they got together again a year later and moved into an apartment.

Donald was concerned that Ken was promiscuous. He was upset when Ken was ticketed by the police for homosexual behavior in a city park. They broke up again. Donald's concern was valid. Ken eventually died of AIDS, in 1993.

During this period, Donald resumed his interest in the occult. He joined a study group that met weekly at a bookstore in Covington. There were five others in the group: Dave and Diane MacDonald, Sharon McGee, and two he knew only as Tom and Lanny. They also met socially at Dave and Diane's house to swim in their pool and grill out. Dave and Diane had a ritual room in their basement, but Donald was not included in any of their ceremonies because he had not been initiated. He met with the group in Covington for about a year. Ken accompanied him to the meetings a couple of times but was not a regular member of the group.

Donald began taking a correspondence course in witchcraft from Gavin and Yvonne Frost, a couple in New Bern, North Carolina, with the intent of becoming eligible for initiation. He completed his course in June 1977 and was ready for initiation; but he had a problem. The Frosts would initiate members into their coven only in couples—and his partner had to be a woman. Donald, now openly homosexual, had no suitable relationship with any woman. The Frosts did not know that Donald was homosexual and would not have accepted him into the coven had they known.

Thinking that Donald's problem was only that he had no female partner interested in witchcraft, the Frosts provided a solution. Jan,* a twenty-three-year-old nursing assistant living in Boston, was also a candidate for initiation. Donald and Jan both flew to New Bern for the initiation.

For the ceremony, they were joined by Bill* and Alice,* a local couple who were members of the coven. The four of them went to the Frosts' house for dinner. After dinner, they enjoyed a glass of homemade mead before proceeding to the living room, where the Frosts had removed the furniture and set up an altar. Yvonne, as high priestess, conducted the initiation. During the initiation, Donald met Duncan, a doctor who had been killed in World War II, and accepted him as his otherworld spiritual guide.

In the final step of the initiation, Donald and Jan had to switch partners with Bill and Alice and to have sexual intercourse. They went into separate bedrooms. Alice told Donald that after the birth of their third child, Bill had a vasectomy, but she continued to take birth control pills although Bill could not impregnate her. She didn't want to use a condom, even though they were to collect the sperm for the ceremony. She said she would spit in a condom and pass that off. After they had intercourse twice, she admitted to Donald that she had been off the pill for several months.

The next day, Jan told Donald that Bill had been unable to maintain an erection long enough to complete the sex act and that he had spit in the condom to simulate it. Donald thought it a good joke that Bill and Alice were both spitters.

The new initiates flew to their homes and never saw each other again, although they talked to each other by telephone off and on for several years.

Donald says that several months later, Alice called him with the news that she was pregnant and he was the father. She said that Bill was not dealing with that well, but she had always wanted a fourth child. When she was about six months pregnant, she left Bill and moved to Missouri. Bill stayed in North Carolina with the three children. Alice had a son born in Missouri, but Donald has never seen him.

---

*fictitious names

11. A Fresh Start

Donald had a dilemma. His job as a clerk at St. Luke Hospital was not satisfying, but his best opportunity for a good job was to use his nursing experience. To list his employment at Marymount on an application was to invite inquiry he wanted to avoid.

He decided to take the chance. No one had raised any questions about the deaths at Marymount. No mention of his off-the-job troubles would be on any official hospital records. The laws designed to protect the innocent would also protect the guilty, especially since the sisters were so concerned about lawsuits. They would confirm his employment dates and position and indicate that he had resigned for personal reasons. In an interview, he would say he had resigned to enlist in the Air Force.

He applied for a position at the VA hospital in Cincinnati. Although he had worked as a volunteer at the VA hospital in Lexington, he could not be hired there because of a policy against employing anyone who had been a patient.

The VA took seven months checking references. They apparently followed a thorough bureaucratic routine that failed to elicit the pertinent information. Donald sought help from former Governor Louie B. Nunn to obtain the release required because he had received psychiatric care at the VA hospital in Lexington. He was finally offered a position as a nursing assistant in September 1975.

He resigned from his clerical job at St. Luke Hospital in order to accept the nursing job at the VA hospital. After several months, he shifted to the housekeeping department as a janitor, because the pay and the work schedule were better. He worked there for a year and a half, six months of that time on loan to the VA nursing home in Fort Thomas, Kentucky, in the same capacity.

Harvey was classified as a "critical care" janitor. That meant he worked in the ward where patients were in critical condition, expected to die. The staff called the ward "death alley." Harvey felt sorry for the patients. They had no hope of getting better, and some were in pain. Although he had no direct responsibility for patient care, he had access to them because of his duties, and no one questioned his being in their rooms.

Joseph C. Harris, still in his forties, was dying of cirrhosis of his liver. He was in a lot of pain. He had difficulty breathing and was receiving oxygen through a nasal tube. Harvey adjusted the oxygen flow to a lower setting. Sometime between the end of Harvey's shift and his return the next day, Harris died. Harvey believes his action in reducing the oxygen flow was the cause of Harris's death.

James A. Twitty, James R. Ritter, Harry Rhodes, and Sterling Moore died in the terminal care ward while Harvey was working there. Harvey believes he was responsible for their deaths, although he cannot remember details. He said he turned things off and pulled electrical plugs part way out of their sockets. He remembers that at least once he injected air into a patient's vein with a hypodermic syringe. He also remembers "messing around" with Twitty's IV, but he does not know whether that was a factor in his death. He thinks he smothered Moore with a pillow. He said he was probably responsible for other deaths that he doesn't remember, because he has guilt feelings.

During an interview in 1987, police read to him a list of patients who had died in the VA hospital during that time, but Harvey could not remember doing anything to hasten their deaths.

Harvey was transferred to the pathology department as an autopsy attendant in March 1983. He didn't like the term "diener," which was commonly applied to this position, because he felt it was degrading. (*Diener* is a German word for servant.) During his work in the pathology department, he learned much about anatomy and about the autopsy process. As part of his training, he worked weekends as an autopsy assistant at Christ Hospital in Cincinnati for eight months.

He was transferred in May 1984 to the cardiology catheterization laboratory as a technician. He prepared patients for the procedure and conducted treadmill stress tests, monitoring the tests with EKGs.

On September 19, 1984, Harvey made a fatal error. Hiram Proffit, a man in his fifties, was in the catheterization laboratory for a test. As part of the procedure, Harvey administered a dose of heparin. By mistake, he put out the wrong dosage—25,000 units instead of 5,000. Proffit bled to death in the operating room. Harvey discovered his error after Proffit had died. He told no one about his error, and it was not detected.

In March 1985, Harvey was promoted to morgue supervisor. In this capacity, he received bodies and checked their identification records and the autopsy permits. The autopsies were very thorough. From each body autopsied, forty-five to fifty specimens were taken for pathological examination. Donald enjoyed finding that physicians had made mistakes.

While he was working at the VA hospital, Donald joined the National Socialist Party (neo-Nazi) group headed by Robert Brandon of Mason, Ohio. Donald had been interested in Hitler and had read and studied about him. When he read in a newspaper about an upcoming rally, he attended. He saw someone there whom he knew and asked him about the organization. He was invited to a meeting.

The organization was extremely secretive. Donald said there were about twenty in the group, but they did not know each other's names. He himself used the alias Frederick Lampsat. He wanted a "good German" name and appropriated the name of a former neighbor. He was also known by the nickname, "The Butcher," because he worked in the morgue, although no one in the group knew that he was a murderer, and he never killed anyone through or because of any activity of the group.

They held regular meetings at Brandon's house and at the house of Gilbert Smith in Delhi. Sometimes the group met at Donald's house. He was impressed to meet David Duke, former grand wizard of the Knights of the Ku Klux Klan, at one meeting.

Donald engaged with them in handing out flyers and painting messages on walls, including spray-painting the word *Jude* (German for Jew) on the wall of a Jewish temple in Jamestown, Ohio. The temple was unused and undergoing repair at the time. He attained the rank of major in the organization.

He concealed his homosexuality from the Nazis, because he knew that would not be acceptable to them. He was a member for about seven years, breaking his ties with the organization in 1983.

Donald recently declared that he was never a sympathizer with anything the neo-Nazi party stood for. He said he joined in order to gather information to pass on to some friends who were working to destroy the party. Although that claim has not been substantiated and is hardly credible, his joining may well have been a search for connectedness without any real attachment to the cause, like his temporary memberships in various religious organizations.

Donald had an extensive collection of books. A look at a selection of titles may be revealing.

Anonymous, *A Book of Pagan Rituals*, Samuel Weiser, New York, N.Y., 1978

Buckland, Raymond, *The Tree: The Complete Book of Saxon Witchcraft*, Samuel Weiser, New York, N.Y., 1974

Buckland, Raymond, *Practical Candleburning Rituals*, Llewellyn Publications, St. Paul, Minn., 1976

Crowther, Arnold and Patricia, *The Secrets of Ancient Witchcraft with the Witches Tarot*, University Books, Secaucus, N.J., 1974

DeHaan, Richard. W., *Satan, Satanism, and Witchcraft*, Zondervan, Grand Rapids, Mich., 1972

de Purucker, G., *Occult Glossary*, Theosophical University Press, Pasadena, Cal., 1972

Farrar, Janet and Stewart, *A Witches Bible, Volume I: The Sabbats*, Magickal Childe, New York, N.Y., 1984

Farrar, Janet and Stewart, *A Witches Bible, Volume II: The Rituals*, Magickal Childe, New York, N.Y., 1984

Fodor, Nandor, *The Haunted Mind*, Helix Press, Garrett Publications, New York, N.Y., 1959

Huson, Paul, *Mastering Witchcraft*, Berkley Publishing Corporation, New York, N.Y., 1970

Martello, Leo L., *Understanding the Tarot*, Castle Books, HC Publishers, Secaucus, N.J., 1972

Rockwell, George Lincoln, *White Power*, Liberty Bell Publications, Reedy, W.Va., 1967

12. A Dysfunctional Partnership

Donald was now openly homosexual. He claims to have had between fifty and one hundred sexual partners by the time he was twenty-eight years old. Almost all were casual contacts, as many as five in one night. Donald says these were just for sex, and there was no emotional involvement.

They did not exchange full names in these pickup encounters. He often made up a name instead of using his own. He liked the aggressive role, but he was willing to be the receptive partner also.

After work he hung around gay bars in Clifton, the university area of Cincinnati. At this time, Donald was living alone. One of his favorite hangouts was the Golden Lion. He often went there with Doug Hill, whom he dated off and on for about six years. They had no steady relationship, but they were regular sex partners.

Doug participated with Donald in occult rituals. He was the only person Donald ever permitted to be present when he used the skull. Doug was not a serious believer, but he knew the rituals and would follow them.

Doug was hot-tempered, and they had violent disagreements that never lasted long. One night, after a particularly big argument, Doug chased Donald with his car in the parking lot of the Golden Lion. Donald thinks Doug was just trying to scare him, but he was hit a glancing blow and scraped his leg. Doug apologized and took him home to bandage his leg.

They ostensibly forgave each other, but Donald retaliated by slipping arsenic into Doug's ice cream. The next day Doug's mother called Donald to tell him that Doug was in the hospital with appendicitis. Donald visited Doug in the hospital. Doug recovered. Donald doesn't know whether the contaminated ice cream precipitated the appendicitis attack or not. He wasn't suspected of causing the illness.

At the Golden Lion, Donald met Carl Hoeweler, proprietor of Carl's Coiffeurs, who was there with Diane Alexander, one of his hairdressers and assistant manager. Carl was six feet tall, with bleached blond hair and a mustache. He had an arrogant manner that was attractive to Donald. Although Carl was with Diane, Donald knew he was homosexual, because he had been one of Doug's sex partners. Carl called Donald into the restroom. They went out to Donald's car, where they engaged in sex.

They exchanged telephone numbers, and Carl phoned Donald to ask him to go out with him the next night. They saw each other every night for the next six weeks.

Carl owned a two-family building, and on August 1, 1980, Donald moved in with him. Carl's apartment was decorated in Queen Anne style throughout. Carl was critical of Donald's taste in furniture, so Donald sold most of what he had. He and Carl started to dress alike, and they wore wedding bands. They settled into a pattern of living. Donald cooked for both of them and mowed the lawn. They went out to dinner often, liking particularly the Golden Lamb in Lebanon, the Twenty-Mile House, Prime & Wine, and Skyline Chili.

Donald considered Carl a lot of fun to be with. They enjoyed movies together. Carl gave Donald expensive gifts. Donald thought that Carl felt superior to him, but he could manipulate Carl.

When Carl was arrested for indecent public exposure, Donald learned that he had a practice of going to a public park on Mondays, his day off, to play around with other homosexual men. Donald started feeding him small doses of arsenic on Sundays to make him sick on Mondays. He put the arsenic in Carl's coffee or sprinkled it on his food. A pinch was enough to cause diarrhea.

Donald had read about arsenic through his work at the laboratory at the VA hospital and kept an unlabeled bottle of an arsenic compound in the basement. He experimented on himself to determine a dosage that would have the effect he wanted without being fatal. Carl developed symptoms of chronic arsenic poisoning that Donald could recognize, such as striation in his fingernails and numbness in his feet.

Carl went to many doctors and underwent numerous tests, trying to discover the reason for his illness. The doctors finally concluded that the cause was exposure to chemicals used in hairdressing. Donald derived extra pleasure from having fooled the doctors.

Donald was careful to keep the doses small, just enough to make Carl sick, not enough to kill him. He loved Carl and felt that he was making him sick for his own good—to keep him out of trouble. But he did want him to suffer, because he felt Carl was being unfair to him. Donald had given up his way of life and his friends for Carl, but Carl had not made the same commitment to him.

In some ways, Carl, Donald, and Diane were a threesome. Although they were often together, she was never involved in sex with either of them. Diane was grossly overweight and waddled when she walked. Donald considered her a fag hag. Carl and Donald would go to her house for dinner on Wednesdays, and she would come to Carl's on Thursdays and Fridays. Donald cooked the dinners for the three of them at Carl's. Donald and Diane were jealous of each other and engaged in petty sniping and bickering. She acted friendly to Donald in front of Carl, but not in Carl's absence. Donald felt she was trying to split up Carl's relationship with him. He decided to get rid of her.

One of Donald's duties at the morgue of the VA hospital was to dispose of waste from the laboratory. He centrifuged a sample of blood from a patient with hepatitis B and took the clear serum home. He mixed the serum into Diane's salad dressing.

Diane did develop hepatitis. At first her illness was misdiagnosed, and she was treated for gall bladder problems, then pancreatitis. Again Donald enjoyed having the doctors stumped, feeling superior because he knew what was really wrong with her.

Donald also poisoned Diane with acrylic acid, which he added to her soft drinks. The acrylic acid caused her hands and feet to swell. Donald wanted her to suffer. He tried unsuccessfully to infect her with AIDS virus obtained from the laboratory.

Donald is convinced that during the time that he was poisoning Carl and Diane, both of them were also administering small doses of some kind of poison to him, which caused frequent bouts of diarrhea. They never confronted each other about their suspicions that each was poisoning the other.

Donald cooked a large batch of beef stroganoff for a dinner party at Carl's house during the Christmas season. The stroganoff sat out for several hours at the party, and the leftovers were put in the freezer. The leftovers were thawed and reheated twice. The second time was for a dinner party Carl gave at his house for the women who worked as hairdressers in his shop. Donald sprinkled arsenic on top of the stroganoff that night.

Everyone at the party except Donald and Carl, who ate none of the stroganoff, got sick, and several were taken to the hospital to have their stomachs pumped. The illnesses were attributed to food poisoning. Donald's addition of arsenic was never suspected. When Donald told investigators about the incident years later, he said that the arsenic wasn't a factor, because he had sprinkled on "only a little."

Helen Metzger occupied the second floor of Carl's building. She was a very active, outgoing person, but she was going blind from glaucoma and was upset about it. She and Donald were on good terms, and Donald would take her leftovers from meals he had prepared for himself and Carl.

Helen became curious about money that Carl was spending on remodeling and questioned Donald about it several times. Donald told her that he did not know where the money was coming from and that he was not interested; but she persisted in inquiring about it. Donald considered her a threat to Carl and indirectly to him.

He decided to give her arsenic in the leftovers. He gave her what he considered a small dose in a stew and put some in a jar of mayonnaise. Several weeks later he gave her another dose in a pie. He didn't think he was giving her a lethal dose, but she developed a paralysis that began with her feet and progressed upward. She had extreme difficulty in breathing, requiring a tracheotomy. Following the tracheotomy, she started hemorrhaging and never regained consciousness. Her death was attributed to Guillain-Barré Syndrome. Homicide was not suspected.

Donald is unable to say whether his decision to poison her was because of feeling sorry for her or because he thought her inquisitiveness about the money was a threat to Carl. He said he was relieved when she died. He was a pallbearer at her funeral.

The mayonnaise containing arsenic was still in Helen Metzger's refrigerator after she died. When the family gathered in her apartment after her funeral, someone made some tuna salad using the mayonnaise. Four of the women became ill, but no one made the connection between their illness and her death. All four recovered.

Henry Hoeweler, Carl's father, was a patient at Mercy Franciscan Hospital

Mt. Airy, then known as Providence Hospital. He had only one kidney and was suffering from congestive heart failure. Donald visited him in the hospital as a friend, not in any official capacity. Hoeweler told him that he wanted to die. Donald fed him a dose of arsenic. He had planned to give him another dose; but two days later, when drinking a milkshake that Carl had brought him, Henry Hoeweler had a stroke. He died four days later as a result of the stroke and kidney failure.

Donald claims that another death in Carl's family, that of Howard Vetter, Carl's brother-in-law, was accidental, and the official conclusion was in agreement. On Christmas Eve, Donald was cleaning newly installed windows in Carl's house using wood alcohol to remove adhesive labels from the glass. He kept the alcohol in a vodka bottle. He put the bottle in a storage area for odds and ends near the bar. When Vetter came over to the house, Carl somehow got hold of the wrong bottle and served him two drinks made with the wood alcohol. Vetter was sick for a week, and on New Year's Eve suffered a heart attack. While undergoing tests at Good Samaritan Hospital, he died. His death was attributed to cardiac failure. Although this was technically a "coroner's case," because of the circumstances, there was no autopsy. His death was declared an accident.

James Peluso re-entered Donald's life when he came to the VA hospital as a patient with a very bad heart. He came to visit Donald several times at Carl's house. Peluso wanted to tell Carl about their fifteen-year off-and-on affair. Donald objected, but he feared Peluso would tell Carl anyway.

Peluso told Donald that if he ever became unable to care for himself, he wanted Donald to "help him out," which Donald interpreted as meaning a painless death. Donald gave him arsenic in a daiquiri, and another time in some pudding. Peluso became ill again at home and was taken back to the VA hospital, where he died. His death was expected because of his cardiac problems, so no autopsy was performed.

Edward Wilson and his wife, Mary, moved into the apartment vacated when Helen Metzger died. He was in his eighties, and Donald said, "He was the nicest old man you would ever want to meet." Donald felt sorry for him, too, because he had a bad case of shingles. He was invited to a wedding, but he wouldn't go because the shingles disfigured his face. Donald also thought that Wilson's daughter was not good to him.

Wilson became upset about his utility bills and claimed that Carl was cheating him. Thinking he was acting to protect Carl, Donald gave the

Wilsons arsenic in food. He also put arsenic in a bottle of Pepto Bismol he found in the Wilson's medicine cabinet. Both Wilsons became ill, but only Edward took the medicine. He died five days later. There was an autopsy, but the arsenic was not discovered.

Donald had also poisoned the Wilsons's dog with arsenic because she attacked his dog. The Wilsons's dog was old and had been sick a lot, with many trips to the veterinarian, so her death raised no suspicions.

In July 1985 the security staff at the VA hospital, acting on an anonymous tip, stopped Donald and made him show them the contents of a gym bag he was carrying. In the gym bag, they found a loaded .38 caliber pistol—a clear violation of policy. They also found books from the library. The pistol belonged to Donald, but he denies that he ever carried it to work intentionally. He also insists that he had a right to have the books, because he was permitted to take them home to study.

They also searched his locker and found a small specimen of liver mounted in paraffin wax to be sliced with a microtome for microscopic examination. Donald said he had the sample for a course in histology he was taking to qualify for promotion.

Donald, being a supervisor, had no protection from the union and was fired summarily. Because the investigation was not executed properly, violating Donald's rights, none of these events appeared on his record. Security Chief Daniel Wilson was disciplined for mishandling the case.

There were rumors, never substantiated, that Donald had organs taken from the morgue to be used in witchcraft. (See chapter 4.)

Donald believes that Carl had planted the gun in his satchel and was the source of the anonymous tip, because the two had returned from a vacation in Florida at odds over events there. Carl denied Donald's accusations, but their relationship was never the same after this incident.

13. Terminal Care

Although Donald Harvey had left positions at two hospitals under clouds of suspicion, his record looked good on paper. He had been allowed to resign from Marymount, and the events leading up to his resignation had not been added to his employment record. Procedural errors had caused details of his firing from the VA hospital to be suppressed.

He applied for a position as nursing assistant at Daniel Drake Memorial Hospital in Cincinnati on December 5, 1985. The red brick five-story hospital, built in 1952, looked its age. This Hamilton County facility, operated with tax funds, provided essential long-term nursing and rehabilitation services for medically indigent adults.

He spent half a day at the hospital with Daisy Key, the head nurse on the ward then called B-100, meeting the staff on both the day and evening shifts. He made a good impression. Key recommended employment, commenting favorably on his hospital experience.

Within a week he received a telephone call offering him a position. He started to work on February 24, 1986. After a three-week training period to familiarize him with that particular hospital and its procedures, he was qualified to work in the hospital section, skilled nursing care, and rehabilitation.

He was assigned to a ward in skilled nursing care. Although he liked working with patients, he found the assignment depressing. The patients were in long-term care, with little expectation of ever leaving Drake alive. Most were hardly conscious. Harvey felt sorry for them and for their families, whom he would see visit and just sit in the rooms looking forlorn. He felt that death would be a relief for everyone concerned.

Harvey did not like Nathaniel Watson, an African-American man age sixty-five, who was in a semi-comatose state being fed with a gastric tube. Harvey later told an interviewer that he didn't agree with feeding a vegetable who ought to be dead. Harvey's antipathy stemmed from being told that Watson was a convicted rapist, brought to the hospital from a county jail. Harvey attributes many of his own problems to having been raped when he was a child.

The rumor was quite likely false. Watson had been head of nutritional services at Jewish Hospital until seven years before, when he had been diagnosed as having a brain tumor and became partially paralyzed as a result of surgery to remove the tumor. His wife, Jean, who was a nurse, had cared for him at home until he had a stroke and required hospital care.

Watson lay most of the time in a fetal position. He had no use of his hands or arms. Although Watson showed no response to most stimuli, Harvey believes he had some awareness, because he would get a semi-erection when one of the female nurses would work on him. He could also follow movement with his eyes. Harvey said that he could sometimes see anger in those eyes.

Early in the afternoon of a Monday in April, Harvey entered room B-107, which Watson shared with four other patients. He greeted him, "Mr. Watson, how are you today?" Of course, Watson could not answer. Harvey pulled the curtains around his bed. He washed his patient's face and changed his position in the bed. Watson had to be turned every two hours, because he was unable to shift himself.

Harvey took a plastic garbage can liner, wet it, and lay it over Watson's face, pushing it into his mouth and up his nostrils. He checked Watson's heartbeat with a stethoscope, noting that the beats were growing fainter. Hearing a noise in the hall, he quickly removed the plastic sheet and disposed of it in the garbage can. He left the room.

Harvey returned to Watson's room before the end of his shift and repeated the same procedure with another sheet of plastic. He was again interrupted.

The next day, at about the same time, Harvey placed a trash can by the door of Watson's room so that he would have a warning if anyone was entering. He again pulled the curtains around the bed. He wet a sheet of plastic and placed it over Watson's face, pushing it into his mouth and nostrils to shut off his air supply. Then he laid a pillow over the plastic. He observed that

Watson started to sweat and take on an ashen hue. With his stethoscope, he listened to Watson's heartbeat as it slowed and stopped after about three minutes. He waited beside the bed for two more minutes, alert to remove the pillow and dispose of the plastic bag should he hear anyone approaching.

When he was sure Watson was dead, he removed the pillow and threw the plastic bag in his garbage cart. Then he went on to wash his next patient's face and put a clean gown on him.

Three-quarters of an hour later, Sherry Rudd (no relation to Margaret Rudd), the nurse on duty, discovered that Watson was dead. Donald helped her prepare his body for the morgue and straighten the room.

There was no autopsy, and foul play was not suspected.

14. Expanding Fatal Skills

Harvey felt sorry for Leon Nelson, a sixty-four-year-old man who had been brought to Drake Hospital when he slipped into a coma after two surgical operations for a brain cyst. Nelson was paralyzed; he had no use of his limbs. He was semi-conscious, and his eyes were closed. He was probably aware, but he was unable to respond to any stimuli except for mumbling one or two words. He was not a candidate for rehabilitation. Harvey considered him easy to care for, because he lay flat on his back. He was fed with a gastric tube and had a nasal tube to assist in his breathing.

About a week after Nathaniel Watson's death, Harvey decided to end Nelson's life. He followed the same procedure he had used for smothering Watson. Harvey left him and went on to his other duties. Sherry Rudd found Nelson dead, and Harvey helped her prepare his body for the morgue. He had some concern about being caught for killing Nelson, because Nelson had all the symptoms of smothering, which Harvey had learned from Vern Midden. But no suspicions were raised.

Harvey liked Virgil Weddle, a white man who was eighty-one years old. They talked when Harvey was taking care of him, because Weddle was from Danville, Kentucky, close to the area in which Harvey grew up. Weddle had severe heart problems and was suffering. He prayed to die.

Having made a decision to grant Weddle's prayer, Harvey went to Central Hardware near the Northgate shopping mall in the northwestern part of Hamilton County and examined a package of rat poison that he thought contained arsenic. The label said the poison would cause hemorrhaging and a painless death. Harvey bought the rat poison and put a small portion in a vial, which he took to work with him the next day.

He thought from his experience in giving arsenic to Carl that killing Weddle would require several doses of the poison. He prepared the first dose by mixing about a teaspoonful into a green pistachio pudding. Weddle was sitting in the hall outside his room. Harvey fed him lunch, saving the pudding for last. Before Harvey had fed him half the pudding, Weddle started having trouble breathing. Harvey stopped a nurse and the two of them tried to return Weddle to his bed, but he collapsed and died within about ten minutes. During the commotion, Harvey slipped Weddle's food tray with the uneaten portion of the pudding back onto the food cart. Sherry Rudd was again the nurse on duty.

Harvey was not concerned about the possibility of an autopsy. Weddle had died of an apparent heart attack, which was the expected outcome of his illness. Harvey was relieved that Weddle was out of his misery.

Weddle's wife, Geneva, had been friendly with the staff at the hospital. She returned after his death and had a small luncheon in appreciation for the staff members who had cared for her husband.

Harvey had made a mistake in thinking that the rat poison contained arsenic. The active ingredient was almost certainly Warfarin, a powerful blood thinner. So Weddle's death was probably actually from a heart attack, possibly triggered by the effect of the Warfarin.

The day after Weddle died, Harvey added a dose of the rat poison to pudding served to Lawrence Berndsen, a man in his sixties slowly recovering from a stroke. Berndsen showed no immediate reaction, but he developed diarrhea and the symptoms of his stroke became worse—more drooping of his mouth and slurring of his speech. Over a period of several days, Harvey repeated the administration of the rat poison with similar results. Berndsen was transferred to a nursing home and died there. There was no way to determine whether Harvey was responsible for his death.

Donald's relationship with Carl was deteriorating. Donald resented Carl's arrogance, and he objected to being told what to do. Carl told him, "I picked you out of the gutter, and I can put you back there." Their friction escalated, and on May 2, 1986, they quit being lovers, although Donald continued to live in Carl's house.

Doris Nally, a sixty-five-year-old white woman, had retired from U.S. Shoe Company after thirty-five years of service. She had been transferred to

Drake from Providence Hospital, diagnosed as being terminally ill with lung cancer that metastasized to her brain. She was very thin and totally dependent for all elements of daily living. Harvey was working the seven-to-three shift on Friday, May 2. Nally's daughter, one of her three children, was visiting her that afternoon. About two o'clock, during a temporary absence of the daughter, Harvey gave Nally about a quarter of a teaspoonful of cyanide in about one hundred cubic centimeters of apple juice and helped her to drink it. When Nally's daughter returned, she observed that her mother was not feeling well and left her to rest. Nally was found dead on the next shift.

On May 5, 1986, head nurse Daisy Key completed an employee performance evaluation for Donald Harvey. She rated his performance good on six of ten criteria, and acceptable on the other four. Her comments were: "Donald's attitudes toward his job and patients and staff are good. Cooperation good. Keeps his team leader informed. Attendance and punctuality good. Makes suggestions and offers help to team members. Has completed two parts in his orientation program to assist in autopsy with Dr. Pappas when needed. Received good reports."

Harvey had a supply of arsenic he had taken from the VA laboratory when he worked there. Several weeks after he had fed the rat poison to Weddle, he used some of the arsenic to cause another death. His victim was Edward Schreibeis, who was in his sixties. Schreibeis was alert, but unable to speak. Harvey felt sorry for him. He gave him a large dose in his soup. Schreibeis became critically ill and was moved to the hospital floor, where he died some days later. There was no autopsy.

Harvey gave arsenic to Willie Johnson, fifty-nine, four times in his food during May and June 1986. Each time Johnson vomited up the poison. Johnson, who survived, had no idea that Harvey had tried to poison him.

When Daisy Key completed Harvey's next performance evaluation report, on June 24, she raised his rating on all criteria to good, except for one item, judgment, which she rated as acceptable. Her comments included: "Donald is motivated and works well with staff. Gives good patient care. Good attitude toward unit and assignments and patients and families. . . . Skills check list completed."

Arsenic wasn't the only poison Harvey had taken from the VA laboratory. He also had a bottle of cyanide crystals. He started carrying a small vial of cyanide solution to work, just in case he wanted to use it. He sometimes acted on impulse without any signal from his otherworld guide, Duncan.

Robert Crockett, an eighty-year-old African-American, was brought to Drake in what Harvey was sure was a terminal condition. He suffered from numerous large bedsores and was unable to communicate. His diagnosis was "severe organic brain syndrome." He had sepsis and recurrent urinary infections.

Crockett was being given an IV. Harvey withdrew half the contents of his vial of cyanide solution into a hypodermic syringe. He injected the contents of the syringe into the Y of Crockett's IV. Crockett's breathing became very shallow, and he turned ashen. Harvey left the room.

The nurse on duty, Joyce Buchanan, found Crockett expiring. She called the doctor; but Crockett had been designated "no code," which meant that no extraordinary means would be employed to resuscitate him. Harvey helped transfer Crockett's body to the morgue. He removed and discarded the IV tubes, which was standard procedure. Permission for an autopsy was not granted.

The day was June 29, 1986. Donald had been employed at Drake for four months. During that time he had caused the deaths of six patients and attempted to murder two others. He was unaware that some of the nurses had begun to talk about him behind his back, speculating that there were an abnormal number of deaths among his patients. He was cautious about his lethal activities, but his experiences at Marymount and the VA hospital had led him to feel invulnerable.

Donald bought a mobile home, and on August 17, he moved from Carl's house to a lot in Middletown, Ohio.

15. A Killing Routine

Donald Barney, sixty-one, a single white man, was a victim of a street mugging. He had a subdural hematoma with seizures and suffered from dementia. He was barely aware of anything around him. He could not move his limbs voluntarily and was unable to talk, although his eyes were able to follow movement.

Barney had been in hospitals and nursing homes since May 1981. On January 24, 1985, he had been transferred to Drake from the University of Cincinnati Medical Center for skilled nursing care. At that time, Dr. Verma reported that his overall prognosis was poor and he had no rehabilitation potential.

He was fed through a gastric tube. He had multiple severe bedsores and was in isolation because of a staph infection. His condition was gradually becoming worse. In addition, a lump was arising on the side of his face, and a biopsy was scheduled. Harvey had a mistaken idea that the doctor had recommended surgery to remove the lump and that Barney's mother had refused permission.

At the staff meeting on July 7, 1986, nurse Helen Hickneyer reported that Barney's condition was critical. Harvey was assigned responsibility for his care that shift. Barney had a tracheotomy tube and was constantly producing a mucous. For several days, the mucous had been a sickly green.

Harvey gave Barney cyanide through his feeding tube. He mixed an additional dose of cyanide and injected it under Barney's buttocks on his left side. Barney had a respiratory shutdown and died in about five minutes. Harvey left the room, because he did not want to be the one who discovered that Barney was dead. Helen Hickneyer found him dead more than two hours later when she came around to give him medication.

The site of the injection turned black, but only Harvey observed that, as the injection was close to a bed sore. Because Barney was a coroner's case as a result of the mugging, an autopsy was performed, but the bedsores camouflaged the injection site. His death was recorded as due to sepsis and pneumonia.

James Woods, an African-American in his sixties, was retired from General Electric. He had suffered a stroke, but he was aware of his surroundings. He had a G-tube and a tracheotomy tube. Harvey put a cyanide solution in Woods's gastric tube. Woods soon went into respiratory arrest, but a nurse working with another patient in the same room discovered his condition. Woods was a code patient, so they used the crash cart and resuscitated him. The paramedics were called to take him to Good Samaritan Hospital, but he died there several days later.

Earnest Frey had Alzheimer's disease. He thought Harvey was one of his friends, Bill or David, from the distant past. Harvey liked Frey and enjoyed talking with him, and he was bothered that no one ever came to visit. Frey was more than eighty years old. He could stand with assistance, but he could not walk. He was fed through a gastric tube. The Shriners' Circus was in town, and Frey was taken to the show. Harvey thinks that was a bad mistake, because Frey was seeing pink elephants when they brought him back. That night Harvey put arsenic in his gastric tube. He vomited, and Harvey detected a sweet odor. Frey was moved to the hospital unit, where he died several days later. Harvey knew there would be an autopsy for research purposes, but he was not afraid that the arsenic would be detected. He was familiar with the pathologist's routine, because he had assisted in several autopsies at Drake.

Harvey liked Milton Canter, a Jewish man who was eighty-five years old. Canter could talk, and he and Harvey discussed baseball. However, Harvey considered Canter's family a pain, both his wife, Goldie, and his daughter, Connie, whom Donald thought spacey. They had moved into an apartment near the hospital in order to be close to him. Goldie visited her husband early every morning and returned later in the day for another visit. Goldie would insist on getting him up, even when she was going to be there only a few minutes. Canter was sometimes out of his head and would pull his tubes out, so it was necessary to tie his hands. Harvey once reported one of the nurses for washing off Canter's gastric tube and reusing it.

Canter had originally been transferred to Drake from Jewish Hospital on May 15, 1986, following a stroke. On July 13 he developed a blood clot in his leg and was returned to Jewish Hospital for surgery. He returned to Drake two days later.

Harvey felt sorry for Canter. On August 29, Canter was being fed through a nasal tube. Harvey mixed a cyanide solution and inserted it into the tube with a syringe. Canter had an instant respiratory shutdown. Harvey pulled the nurse call cord, but there was no response. He later filed a complaint with the nurses' supervisor. Harvey rushed down the hall, calling for a nurse. Although Canter was designated no code, the nurses attempted resuscitation unsuccessfully.

Permission for an autopsy was not granted. His death was recorded as due to a pulmonary embolism.

Years later, when Harvey was being questioned about his activities with the neo-Nazi organization, he was asked if Canter's being Jewish was a factor in deciding to kill him. He declared that he did not know that Canter was Jewish until after he was dead, but it would not have made any difference if he had.

Roger Evans, a seventy-four-year-old African-American, had a long history of cardiopulmonary disease and had suffered a stroke. He had been transferred to Drake from Bethesda Hospital for assessment as a candidate for rehabilitation. The assessment was negative. He could talk, although he was sometimes incoherent. He could sit in a chair if tied to hold him in place. Although he could sometimes feed himself, he also had a gastric tube. He had not been at Drake long, but he showed no improvement and plans were being made for transferring him to a nursing home. After giving him a bath and changing his bed, Harvey put a solution of cyanide into his gastric tube. There was no immediate reaction.

He had proceeded to attend to another patient when Evans went into cardiac arrest. Two nurses rushed in with a crash cart and attempted resuscitation. Evans expired about an hour later. Harvey had some concern when Evans's family gave permission for an autopsy, but the conclusion reached was that Evans had died of a massive heart attack.

Clayborn Kendrick was an attorney, retired from the Ohio State Liquor Control Board, where he was a manager. A sixty-nine-year-old African-

American, he had been at Drake for eight months, transferred from the VA Medical Center. He was a victim of multiple strokes and totally dependent on nursing care. He was legally blind, having no vision in his left eye and very poor vision in his right.

He lay in a fetal position, but had some awareness and could mumble. He had no voluntary arm movement and was fed through a gastric tube. He also had a nasal tube. He was getting worse instead of better. He had numerous infections, especially in his urinary tract. His condition was listed as poor, but he was not thought to be in immediate danger for his life.

Harvey decided to end his suffering, but he delayed action until Kendrick's wife returned from a trip to Hawaii. He didn't want to ruin her vacation. On September 20 Harvey was working a double shift. He closed the curtains around Kendrick's bed, which was standard procedure when working with a patient, and gave him cyanide both in his gastric tube and by injection into his testes. Kendrick developed respiratory distress and died within about fifteen minutes. Harvey called for a nurse, who called their supervisor. Harvey assisted in cleaning up Kendrick's body and transporting it to the morgue. No autopsy was performed. His cause of death was listed as recurrent sepsis.

Over a month elapsed before Harvey killed again. Albert Buehlmann was in the same bed that Kendrick had occupied. A Swiss immigrant, he had Alzheimer's disease and had regressed to speaking in German only. One of the nurses spoke German and could communicate with him a little, but Harvey could not. Buehlmann had little use of his limbs. He had been at Drake for about a month when Harvey decided to end his life. Buehlmann had developed a fever of 104 degrees, and the infection did not seem to respond to antibiotics. His condition was listed as very poor. On that day, Harvey had been responsible for his care. Just before the end of his shift, Harvey dissolved cyanide in a cup of water and held it to Buehlmann's lips. He disposed of the plastic cup in the garbage. There was no immediate reaction, but Buehlmann was dead when Harvey came to work the next day.

William Collins, an African-American ninety years old, was brought to Drake in June 1986 for nursing care related to dementia. He was incontinent and had a history of urinary infections. He suffered from very bad bedsores. Collins was able to talk and to use a wheelchair.

Harvey said that Collins gave up trying to live upon learning that his daughter in Texas had died. Harvey brought cyanide to the hospital and gave it to Collins dissolved in orange juice. He then went to lunch.

Collins vomited and had a respiratory shutdown. A nurse's aide rushed into the room and initiated a code response. Collins was suctioned and given an IV and oxygen. An ambulance was called to transfer him to the University of Cincinnati Medical Center. Cardiac arrest occurred, and the call for an ambulance was cancelled.

When Harvey returned from lunch, he found that Collins had died. There was no autopsy. His death certificate shows "possible myocardial infarction."

Harvey does not remember well the details of the next death, but hospital records indicate that Henry Cody died on November 4, and the circumstances seem to fit Harvey's description of a patient whose name he can't remember. The patient was comatose and couldn't move his limbs.

Cody was a seventy-eight-year-old African-American who had been transferred from Jewish Hospital in moribund condition on October 24. He was being treated with antibiotics for sepsis. At 1:30 A.M. on November 4, his temperature was 106.4 degrees. Harvey added cyanide dissolved in water to his gastric tube just at the end of his shift. Dr. Parikh was called just before 5:00 A.M. and informed that Cody had expired. He found the patient was not breathing and could find no pulse. An EKG confirmed death at 5:00 A.M. Cody's wife, Lillie, refused permission for an autopsy. Dr. Parikh recorded that the cause of his death was cardiac arrhythmia. On his death certificate, Dr. Verma reported recurrent pneumonia as the immediate cause.

Donald was depressed about his break-up with Carl. He began receiving treatment by a psychiatrist, Dr. Mark Barbara. He apparently tried to commit suicide by deliberately driving his car off a mountain road, although he claims the mishap was an accident. He received a head injury, but it was not fatal.

Donald has never been able to explain why, when he could kill others efficiently, he bungled three suicide attempts. Asked that question recently, he told the interviewer that he never seriously attempted to kill himself, characterizing his attempts as bids for attention. He said he didn't use a gun, because he had observed in hospitals that people shot in the head didn't necessarily die, and he did not want to live in a vegetative state like some of the patients he had known. He said he knew from experience that an overdose of sleeping pills didn't always work.

Donald's occult rituals were a regular practice, and he sought Duncan's guidance in selecting his victims or, as he would put it, selection of the patients to be relieved of their misery. As he repeated recently, "Remember,

Duncan had been a doctor." He did not consider himself bound by Duncan's selections, however, and responded to opportunities as he encountered them.

Although he had usually brought cyanide to the hospital only when he had a particular patient in mind, by autumn of 1986 he started carrying it every day. He later said he planned to take it himself if he were ever caught and arrested. It is not clear whether fear of getting caught was a conscious concern at the time or is a later rationalization of past behavior.

Harvey felt sorry for Mose Thompson Jr., who was aware, but could not speak. He just lay in bed with a fixed stare, although he was able to communicate with eye blinks in response to simple questions. His limbs were paralyzed. Thompson was a sixty-five-year-old African-American, admitted to Good Samaritan Hospital on September 10, 1986, with a brainstem infarction. He had a history of coronary heart disease and diabetes and had undergone coronary bypass surgery in July 1985. He had been transferred to Drake on September 24. His condition had not improved.

His wife was very religious and read religious literature to him when she visited. A young woman, either his daughter or his granddaughter, also visited him.

Thompson had been at Drake about two months when Harvey decided to end his life. Harvey had not been assigned to care for him that day. In order to limit suspicion, Harvey didn't limit his killing to his assigned patients.

Entering Thompson's room, Harvey found nurse's aide Angie Moeller there. She looked at him with suspicion. "You're in the wrong room."

"Somebody's busy in my rooms, so I thought I'd help out by changing the linens in here and then go to my assigned rooms."

"I can use help." Moeller accepted his explanation and left to see about another patient.

In the process of changing the linens, Harvey stopped long enough to insert a dose of cyanide dissolved in water into Thompson's gastric tube with a syringe. He left the room. Thompson had a respiratory shutdown. Dr. Sarkar pronounced him dead at 8:25 A.M. on November 22. Permission for an autopsy was not granted. The cause of death was listed as cardiac arrhythmia.

Odas Day had been a policeman. He was a white man, seventy-two years old. He had been brought to Drake from Jewish Hospital several months before. His health problems apparently began with smoke inhalation and a heart attack in 1970. His condition had been seriously deteriorating since 1982.

He had a stroke in 1984 and had been dependent on oxygen off and on since then. In the summer of 1986 he was hospitalized several times and had a pacemaker implanted in August of that year. He had chronic heart disease. His circulation, especially in his lower extremities, was poor because of severe peripheral vascular disease.

While he was at Good Samaritan, his feet became gangrenous. Harvey said he was told that Day's legs had been frostbitten by a cooling blanket used in the hospital. Medical records do not support this allegation. The physicians considered amputation but decided not to perform the operation because of his overall poor medical condition. He was classified no code.

He was transferred to Drake for skilled nursing care on September 19, 1986, in a moribund condition. His condition continued to deteriorate slowly. He could talk and had some use of his arms. He could be fed orally, but he was fed through a nasal tube whenever he refused to eat.

On December 9, Day had been in critical condition for several days. He was in a lot of pain. Close to 11:00 P.M. Harvey was putting water in all the bags in that room. He put a cyanide solution in Day's bag and left the room immediately. Day probably died instantly, but his death was discovered about an hour and a half later by a nurse, Rose Valentour. Rose told Harvey, "Thank God he's finally gone." Harvey helped the nurse give postmortem care and take Day's body to the morgue. According to Harvey, Day was at peace, with a smile on his face. Harvey was relieved for him and never thought that he had made a mistake in killing him.

That same morning Harvey was responsible for care of Cleo Fish, a sixty-seven-year-old white woman who was diabetic and partially blind. She had been at Drake since June 8, 1983, having been transferred from University Hospital following a stroke. At first she participated in the rehabilitation program but made little progress because of severe organic brain damage. She was transferred to the skilled nursing facility on February 7, 1985.

Harvey did not like caring for her, because she embarrassed him by playing with her genitals and fondling her own breasts. She objected to male attendants, so Harvey talked to her in a falsetto to conceal that he was a man. He doubts that she was really deceived. She had to have a daily suppository and to have her diaper changed every two hours.

Fish was contradictory. She was often praying to God to "take her home," but she also frequently complained that people were trying to poison her. That morning, about five o'clock, she was talking with Harvey about her children. She told him she wanted to die. Although he had not planned her death in advance, he gave her cyanide mixed into cranberry juice. She had cardiac and respiratory failure, and Harvey called the nurses. Helen and Rose responded.

Helen said, "Well, you killed another one."

Rose objected. "Don't joke about something like that."

Harvey ignored both remarks and helped clean up the body, but he was not the one who took her to the morgue, because he went off duty at seven. No autopsy was performed. Dr. Nascimento recorded her cause of death as sepsis.

Harold White and John Oldendick were more fortunate. Harvey targeted both of them and fed them arsenic, but his doses were too small to be fatal. He was being cautious for fear of detection.

White was diabetic. Harvey thought he would never get better and wanted to put him out of his misery. He gave White arsenic in his food. He threw it up. Harvey planned a second dose, but the doctors got White's diabetes under control.

Harvey fed Oldendick four doses of arsenic over a period of time. He vomited each time and had diarrhea. He seemed to get better after each dose. He was able to leave the hospital and move to a nursing home, where he lived for six months. Harvey thinks that in Oldendick's case the arsenic acted as a medicine and that he actually helped him.

Leo Parker had a brain tumor. Although he could talk and move around, the tumor was growing. He had surgery for the tumor in January 1985 and again in April 1986. He had been in the rehabilitation unit, but he was moved to skilled nursing care.

Parker was younger than the usual patient there, only forty-six. He was African-American. He initially objected to having Harvey provide his care, because he had learned that Harvey was homosexual. He called Harvey a faggot. Their relationship was strained for several days, but Harvey continued to give him care, and Parker came to accept him.

Parker's condition became critical in January 1987. Because of his brain tumor, he was sometimes violent, and he had to be tied in his bed. Harvey decided it was time to end his life. He doesn't think his decision had any relationship to their earlier friction.

Parker could be fed orally, but he also had a nasal tube with a food bag. About 9:40 P.M. on January 10, Harvey put cyanide in his food bag and left to care for another patient in the same room. Parker died soon after, foaming at the mouth. James Hale, another nursing aide, found him dead about eleven o'clock, the end of their shift. He told Harvey, "Let's not report it. I don't want to clean him up for the morgue." Dr. Parikh pronounced him dead at 11:20 P.M., indicating pneumonia as the cause of death. An autopsy failed to find that he had been poisoned.

Margaret Kuckro had been in the hospital for over five years, gradually getting worse. She was a white woman who was seventy-eight years old. She was semicomatose as a consequence of a cerebral hemorrhage. In May 1985, Dr. Verma indicated that Kuckro had no rehabilitation potential and would probably succumb to sepses from repeated urinary tract infections. In May 1986, a mass suspected to be cancerous was found in her left breast. Her family declined any action.

In February 1987, she had a kidney infection that was not responding to medication. She was spoon-fed and had a tremendous appetite. Although she was not on his list of potential victims, Harvey gave her cyanide in orange juice. He gave her the poison about 11:00 P.M. A nurse found her dead two hours later. Permission for an autopsy was not granted. Dr. Parikh recorded the cause of her death as "Cardiac arrhythmia, sudden onset."

On the day before he killed John Powell, Harvey killed Joe Pike by feeding him Detachol, an adhesive remover intended for use with colostomy bags. Harvey knew that Pike was in a terminal condition. He was giving him a bath after feeding him the Detachol, but the nurse told him not to finish, because he was to be moved to the hospital section to die. He died a few hours after the move.

That same day Harvey killed Hilda Leitz by feeding her Detachol through her G-tube. She was a white woman, eighty-two years old, who had been at Drake since 1980, with her condition gradually declining. She had a huge hiatal hernia and reflux esophagitis. In February 1987 she was diagnosed as having pneumonia and was put on oxygen.

Leitz was comatose, but could move one hand a little bit. Harvey gave her the adhesive remover in orange juice. It caused nausea and vomiting, then respiratory failure. A nurse found her dead. She was no code. Harvey had killed three patients in two shifts during which he worked sixteen hours.

Harvey's final victim was Stella Lemon. She was very sick and scared. Harvey had not planned her death, but he gave her cyanide in orange juice at the end of his eleven-to-seven shift. She did not die then, but was moved to the hospital unit, where she died several weeks later—after John Powell.

Harvey usually took something from each patient Duncan had helped him choose for death. The next time he performed his ceremony, he would show the item to Duncan as proof that he had followed Duncan's choice. When he worked at the VA hospital, he usually took a sample of body fluid drawn from the victim—perhaps saliva or a few cubic centimeters of blood.

Later, at Drake, he became more varied in his choice of mementos. From Virgil Weddle, he took some cookies and ate them during the ceremony. From Ernest Frey, he took an old pair of knitted booties. From Milton Canter, he took a lap blanket. He took a lock of hair from Cleo Fish and burned it in a ceremony.

He made a list of his victims at Drake and concealed it behind a picture hanging in his trailer. In the thirteen months that Harvey was employed at Drake Memorial Hospital, he was responsible for twenty-four deaths there.

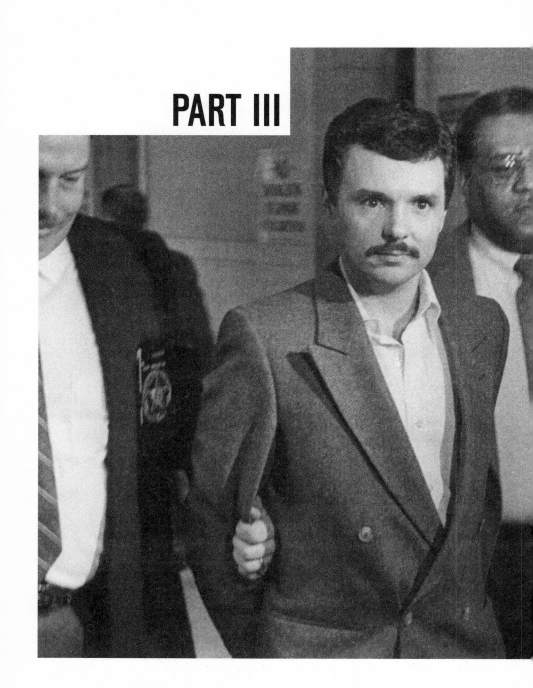

PART III

A REVISED INVESTIGATION

16. Pulling Strings

Donald Harvey was in jail, awaiting trial for the murder of John Powell. Pat Minarcin had broadcast the suggestion that Harvey was responsible for many more deaths at Drake Memorial Hospital. The hospital had vehemently denied that allegation. The county commissioners, responsible for the governance of the county hospital, supported the denial and displayed a letter from the police chief stating that the police had found no evidence of more than one killing. The press and the other television and radio stations, sensing that they had been scooped by Channel 9, were avidly pursuing every possible lead.

Patiently, I led Donald into telling me the whole story. I was amazed at his memory for details of a lifetime of murder. Donald had killed undetected for eighteen years. He left no bloody trails of mutilated bodies, no alarmed citizens, no hue and cry for a serial killer. He killed silently in three hospitals where death was common, choosing victims who were expected to die. He had aroused no hunt for a murderer, because no one had suspected that any of the deaths were not natural. The authorities at the hospitals had a stake in not discovering the murders.

John Powell's murder might easily have slipped into the same category of unquestioned deaths except for the unique set of circumstances. Even then, Powell's death might have been considered an isolated incident had it not been for Minarcin's persistence. But now the hunt was on, even though reluctantly on the part of the authorities. Just one more solid case would warrant a death penalty.

Although the Powell case had yet to come to trial, I was not optimistic about the outcome. Donald had confessed to causing Powell's death, so our only hope for leniency was to portray Donald's action as a mercy killing. But Prosecutor Art Ney, with all the allegations of multiple killings circulating, would put extreme effort into seeing that Donald did not go free.

Donald was reconciled to a prison sentence, but he desperately wanted to avoid the death penalty.

I considered Ney's position. As an elected official, Ney could not risk failing to obtain a conviction of Harvey. He had a strong case on Powell's murder, but without information only Donald could supply, he had nothing substantial on the other cases. Ney had to recognize the possibility that a jury would buy the argument of a mercy killing. On the other hand, I was pessimistic about gambling that none of the other deaths would be discovered independently. If the police could get one more solid case, Donald was doomed. I was anxious to negotiate with Ney while I had some leverage.

From his cell in the justice center, Donald could watch the entrance to the building where the homicide detectives worked. Spying on the activity was a diversion for him. Twice he saw Carl Hoeweler enter the building. On one of those occasions, Carl's car was given a parking ticket while he was inside with the detectives.

Donald told me gleefully what he had observed. I could not join in his fun. I realized that the detectives had sitting in front of them the evidence needed for the second case that would make Harvey eligible for the death penalty. Arsenic accumulates and persists in fingernails and hair. If they even suspected that Donald had been systematically poisoning Hoeweler for years, a simple test for arsenic would have broken the case.

Firmly convinced that a plea bargain was in my client's best interests, I also believed that society would be best served by a lifetime of confinement for Donald. I asked Donald to allow me to offer Prosecutor Ney a remarkable bargain: "If you will agree not to seek the death penalty, Harvey will confess to all his crimes and plead guilty to whatever you indict him for." To avoid the death penalty, Donald agreed.

I called Ney and asked to see him about the Harvey case. Ney agreed to an appointment the next day. First Assistant Prosecutor Carl Vollman was with Ney when I arrived. Since we had worked together for so many years, we chatted amicably for a while. Then, having accomplished the social preliminaries, I got to the point of the visit. "Art, my client is willing to admit that some of the information on the Channel 9 report was true, and there have been other killings. He is willing to give you all the information in exchange for two life sentences, if you will guarantee to grant immunity from any further prosecution on any of the deaths and not to seek the death penalty."

"My first inclination is to seek the death penalty."

"Some of the deaths were outside Hamilton County."

"How many deaths are we talking about?"

I drew a deep breath. "My information is that there may be as many as seventy."

Ney, who had been looking to the side, jerked his head toward me. "Seventy!"

I confirmed the number.

Vollman, silent until this point, entered the conversation. "Give us the names of the victims."

That drew a laugh from me. "Carl, you must think I'm stupid. If I give you the names of the victims, you don't need a plea agreement. You can put my client in the electric chair with that information."

"No, we just want to determine that there is substance to the story."

"Carl, you won't get one piece of information from me until there is an agreement."

They agreed that the prosecutors would think about the offer and that we would meet the next morning to discuss the deal.

17. Plea Bargains

Ten days passed with no response after I had met with Ney and offered the plea bargain. My nervousness was increasing; given enough time the prosecutor might stumble across something that linked Harvey to other crimes. I was now frustrated. Ney was going to let me dangle and ignore my proposition.

I dictated a letter to Ney. My mood had changed, and I was now angry. I didn't want to give Ney any more time. I put the letter in an envelope and personally took it to his office. I told Ney's secretary, Susan, that I had a letter for him, and to make sure that he got it. Mail wasn't fast enough to feed my frustration.

I gave Ney twenty-four hours to respond and declared that if they did not meet that deadline the offer was withdrawn. I was going to bring the matter to a quick conclusion. I was tired of being treated that way and felt I couldn't handle the pressure anymore. I delivered the letter at noon.

I called Minarcin and told him of the letter. Minarcin was dumbfounded. "You must be crazy. They will never agree to that proposal."

He didn't understand the depth of my frustration. Minarcin changed my mood from anger to depression. I had always been told not to undertake a bluff unless I meant to follow through. What if they didn't accept my proposal? Even if I withdrew the proposal, the investigation would continue.

Harvey had to be told of the letter. I went to visit him. The justice center's controlled environment was a relief from the July heat. When I told him, Harvey accepted what had been done. But he asked what would happen if they didn't accept the ultimatum. I couldn't answer. I really didn't know.

That night I tried to concentrate on watching television, but I was unable to do so. At 10:00 P.M., my telephone rang. Terry Gaines, a friend of mine from the prosecutor's office, was on the line. Gaines said that he was in Ney's office, and they had been meeting there all night. He was calling to inform me that we had a deal. He instructed me to be at the office at 8:00 A.M.

I hung up the phone. I had difficulty keeping my feet on the floor. Although Minarcin would be getting ready for the eleven o'clock news, I called him anyway. The operator told me that Minarcin was not available. She asked my name, and upon finding out who I was, asked me to hold a moment.

Minarcin came on the line immediately. "What's up?"

"Pat, you can't put this on the air yet, but I had to tell you. I had a call from Terry Gaines in Art Ney's office. He said Art's going to accept the plea bargain. I'm to be at his office at eight o'clock tomorrow morning."

"Wow! I never thought you could pull it off." His excitement gushed over the line. "You're right. It would be premature to put anything on the air tonight, but call me as soon as you can release it."

I was unable to sleep that night.

The following morning I rushed to the prosecutor's office and was shuttled from the waiting room back through the secretarial pool into the back door to the office of Carl Vollman. I was shocked by the number of people in the room and surprised by who was not there. Vollman was there, with Bill Breyer from the appellate division, Assistant Prosecutors Claude Crowe, Pat Dinkelacker, Terry Gaines, and Joe Deters—all people with whom I had worked closely. Art Ney was not present. My emotions were flip-flopping. These were men I felt very close to, and yet I knew I was now the opposition; we were in an adversarial position.

Deters and Gaines made the prosecutor's position clear. Any agreement would be in writing. Ney was concerned that this was all bravado and insisted on verification of everything. Carl Vollman took me aside and told me Ney wanted to know what hard evidence we could produce to prove that there were other victims. Cornered, I took the risk of mentioning that Harvey had used arsenic, pointing out that they could exhume the bodies of the victims. I used the arbitrary number of three bodies, gambling that without his knowing who the victims were, Ney's hands would be tied. He wouldn't risk the public outcry that would follow digging up everyone who had died at Drake Hospital during that time period, trying to find one of those three. If Ney didn't believe what I was offering, he wouldn't take the risk that he might not find the evidence. To add to Ney's uncertainty, I told Vollman that Harvey's victims had not all been at Drake.

As an extra incentive, I handed Vollman a teaser. I told him that I could produce hard evidence that did not require exhumation. Vollman wanted to know what that evidence was, but I clammed up.

I recognized the negotiating technique being used on me. Anything hammered out by the negotiators was subject to Ney's agreement afterward. It could be said that I had the same advantage; Harvey could refuse to accept something that I had agreed to in the negotiations. But Ney had the position of power. Harvey could only lose.

Joe Deters said, "Art insists on three life sentences, not two."

I resisted, but Joe said, "That one is a deal-breaker. Art will not agree to less."

I conceded reluctantly. We negotiated back and forth, finally agreeing that in exchange for a full confession Harvey would be sentenced to serve three life sentences consecutively, and any additional sentences would be concurrent. The death penalty would be avoided.

In less than two hours a proposed written agreement had been typed and placed in my hand. I was asked to be back at two o'clock having made any corrections I wanted.

Now the weight of the world was on my back again. They had seven or eight brilliant legal minds and I was alone. I called Ray Faller and made arrangements to meet him at one o'clock in the afternoon outside Judge Cartolano's room in the courthouse. Bill Breyer had been in the room. I called Bill's brother, Dan "Woody" Breyer, and he also agreed to meet me outside Cartolano's room.

I had time to kill but didn't know what to do with the time. I couldn't sit still. I went to Cartolano's room and stood outside in the hall. I began going over the document paragraph by paragraph. I found glaring difficulties in several paragraphs, and I made notations. One o'clock came and passed, and no help arrived. I became anxious and agitated. At twenty minutes to two, Woody finally showed up. He perused the agreement and told me he agreed with my changes. Faller didn't appear. Consultation on the plea bargain was outside his earlier agreement with me, and he was tied up in another case. I left to return to the meeting.

I was surprised that most of my changes were readily accepted. However, there were arguments about some of the changes. The proposed agreement stated that if Harvey lied to the prosecutors about any offense, they could negate the whole agreement. I recognized that under those circumstances the prosecution would have the information they sought. They could use it to put Harvey in the electric chair, since he wouldn't be protected by the agreement. I felt that I had to protect Harvey from himself.

I argued about the wording. The prosecutors had inserted a deceptive clause stating that if the agreement were voided, the information supplied by the defendant could not be used in court. But it didn't prohibit other use. I saw the trap—they could use that information to direct a search for evidence that would be admissible. I cited the court rulings in which the evidence commonly called "the fruit of the poison tree" is forbidden. This principle states that information that flows from information obtained illegally is also not admissible. The prosecutors yielded. I concluded that they hadn't expected to get by with that one.

I lost an attempt to delete the word "fraudulent," but I succeeded in having "appears" replaced by "is shown." Another paragraph would void the agreement "if the defendant fails to cooperate fully." I recognized the ambiguity of that provision and insisted that the words "as set out above" be added. The prosecutor's negotiators reluctantly agreed to the revision. I lost an attempt to remove an agreement that the defendant gave up his right to appeal.

One of the men left to have the agreement typed up. Everyone else departed for his or her individual duties, and I was left there alone. I understood why the door was closed; they didn't want anyone to know I was there. As I was sitting alone in that little room, my senses were reeling. Would I get this close to find only frustration? Were they just stringing me along to get more time?

Terry Gaines returned and told me that Ney was reviewing the document before releasing it to me. Shortly thereafter, Joe Deters arrived with the document in hand. He said that I was to get Harvey's signature and return it to them, and Ney would sign it. They wanted to begin taking statements from Harvey the next morning.

I carried the statement to the jail immediately. Joe Deters accompanied me to witness Harvey's signature but stayed out of earshot as I went over the document sentence by sentence with Harvey. I had prepared him well. He had no questions. Without hesitation, he signed it. The agreement was half done. Only Ney's signature was required for completion.

Throughout my representation of Harvey, I had instructed him to have no notes. Now the implementation of the plea was contingent upon his giving everything to the prosecutor. If he left anything out and they found it, they could seek the death penalty. That was an extremely dangerous position, but I could not get the agreement without it. I now needed Harvey to write as much as he could remember. I reversed the instruction to him.

I left the justice center with my heart racing. Harvey was committed to the course of action. I would pull this off if Ney put his signature on the line. My mind was at the same speed as my heart. What if Ney wouldn't sign? What if he changed his mind? He had been known to have second thoughts. What if he upped the ante and wanted additional conditions? Where would I go from there?

My hands left moisture on the doorknob of the prosecutor's office. As instructed, I asked for Joe Deters. He appeared instantly. He took the paper and disappeared down the long hall after telling me to have a seat.

Several prosecutors stopped to talk as they passed in or out of the office. My thoughts diverted, I couldn't get my mind in gear before Joe reappeared with the papers in his hand. He handed the papers to me and directed me to be back in the office the next morning at seven-thirty.

I took the folded white papers from him and walked out, assuring him I would be there as directed. As soon as I was in the hall outside the office, I left the doorway to avoid traffic. Leaning against the wall for support, I opened the papers. My heart raced, for this was the critical moment. Had I succeeded in a big way or in a major flop? The text of the agreement was unchanged. With trepidation, I turned to the last page. Warmth spread throughout my body. My heart rate dropped. Ney's signature was on the line at the bottom of the page.

It was over. While there was a lot of work to do, that was a cakewalk. The difficult portion was past, and I knew I could handle the rest.

It was mid-afternoon; I knew Minarcin would be in his office. I stopped at a pay phone and called. Someone answered and I asked for Minarcin. I was told that Minarcin was busy, but when I gave my name, I was put on hold. Minarcin came on the line. "What's wrong?"

"Can we meet right away?"

We wanted to keep our relationship as secret as we could. Minarcin instructed me to meet him in the garage behind the station.

The station was twelve blocks away. I opted to walk rather than drive. I needed the walk to bring me down to earth. Paranoia had now taken over, and I felt that I was being followed. Several times, I turned around rapidly to find out who was following. I could see no one, but I knew it was just because they were slick. As I was walking on Sixth Street, which took me to the back of the station, several police cars passed. I quickly memorized the car numbers to see if the same cars were coming past again.

I reached the parking lot to the station. I could see the garage; it was still about fifty yards away. I could not see anyone in the area. The summer sun beat down. I had stepped over the chain and taken two steps when a news van pulled into the lot. I stepped back over the chain and stood looking at my watch. There was nothing in the area and no bus stop. I felt that I must look rather stupid, but I didn't know what else to do.

I had to wait for the crew of the van to enter the building, then knocked on the door of the garage. Minarcin immediately opened it. The heat from the garage almost bowled me over. Minarcin was covered with perspiration. He complained of being locked in an oven. Minarcin, at six feet, two inches, towered over me by seven inches.

"What's up?"

Trying to keep a straight face, I pulled the agreement from my pocket and handed it to Minarcin without explanation.

We were both standing in the garage with the door closed. Minarcin was right about the heat, except it was more like being in the steam room at the Y.

Minarcin examined the document closely. I thought of what it would look like if someone walked into the garage. Except for what we were there for, I could think of no legitimate reason for two men to be standing in a heat-baked garage with the door locked.

Minarcin finished the last page. "Goddamn, you did it!" He hugged me in exuberance, and my feet left the ground. Now if someone walked in, he would never believe either of us was heterosexual.

I got out of the hot garage and headed for the justice center. When I met with Harvey to tell him it was a done deal, Harvey produced a multipage document going back eighteen years. He had names, approximate ages, and room numbers. Harvey asked me to take them with me and bring them to the meeting in the morning. I was stunned at what Harvey had accomplished overnight from memory. When I studied the document, I was aghast at the information it contained.

With the plea agreement signed, I believed my job was virtually ended. Harvey's detailed confession and his actual appearance in the courtroom for the formal plea were only formalities. The die was already cast.

I told Harvey, "You understand the requirements of this agreement. You have to cooperate; and if you don't give a complete confession, and they catch you out in anything, they can go after that one more case that, added to Powell, would put you in the electric chair."

Eyes wide, Harvey nodded. "But my memory isn't perfect. There were times I was on medication, and I can't remember everything."

"That's why I had you make this list. Give them everything you can. If you don't know, say so. And don't lie."

"I won't."

"Forget about refusing to answer. That's not available to you . . . about anything in Hamilton County, that is. Don't say anything about Kentucky. That comes under the agreement I'm working out with the Laurel County prosecutor."

"What about deaths outside Drake?"

"Tell them."

"Including the VA?"

"Yes. They can't do anything to you about any deaths covered by the agreement, and that's everything in Hamilton County."

"Some of them, I don't know whether what I did killed them or not."

"Say so. Tell them what you did. It's their job to figure out whether you caused the deaths."

Donald thought that over and nodded slowly. "You'll be with me, won't you?"

"Of course. And you can confer with me at any time. When you want to ask me something, cover your microphone with your hand. You'll be wearing one, and they will be recording everything you say. What you say to me is privileged. They won't risk any violation of your rights, but don't be careless."

"And they really won't give me the death penalty?"

"Not if you stick to the terms of the agreement. It will be three consecutive life terms. That's a minimum of twenty years for each, so that means you can't get out in less than sixty years."

"I'll be ninety-five."

There was one loose thread that had to be dealt with. Harvey had killed patients in Marymount Hospital in Kentucky. While the issue had been ignored during dealing with the deaths in Ohio, I knew that Harvey faced potential danger for the Kentucky deaths. It would take little investigation to determine that Harvey had worked at several hospitals in Kentucky. The deaths at Marymount would surely come to light.

Again, I had the upper hand by knowing where and when the deaths had occurred. Following Harvey's plea, Ney held a press conference in an adjoining building. After Ney appeared and made a statement, I took the podium. Asked whether Harvey had also committed crimes in Kentucky, I refused to acknowledge where and when crimes had occurred, but indicated I was going to initiate contact with the appropriate authorities in Kentucky. Feeling it was only proper to inform the local prosecutor before releasing any information, I returned to his office to drop the bomb.

My call to Tom Handy, the Laurel County prosecutor, was immediately put through. After I introduced myself, Handy asked if Harvey had killed in his jurisdiction. When I acknowledged that was the reason for the phone call, Handy responded, "Wonderful. I was afraid of this." I offered the same deal that had been worked out with Ney: Harvey would cooperate fully in exchange for being spared the death penalty. I asked that Kentucky run the sentences concurrently with the Ohio sentence, with Harvey serving his time in Ohio. Handy promised to get back to me.

Feeling it was Handy's responsibility to release the information, I would not comment further to the media. Members of the press had begun calling each of the commonwealth attorneys of Kentucky asking if theirs was the jurisdiction involved. Each phone call yielded a definite "No" until a call was placed to Tom Handy. Inexperienced with this type of press coverage, Handy was not ready for the news frenzy and answered, "No comment." No more was needed. A rush to the rural county was on.

Handy called Ney to get a solid footing on what he was getting into and to get some idea of what he would be dealing with in a plea bargain with Harvey and me.

I wanted to get that plea agreement signed and settled, but Handy made me wait while he gathered more information.

During all these legal maneuverings outside his presence, Donald never wavered in his regard for me. Later, when he was in prison, he repeatedly expressed his faith in me in his letters. Witness the following excerpts from some of those letters.

AUGUST 22, 1989 – "Dear Bill, I bet there have been days you wish you had called in sick on April 5, 1987. If I don't always say thank you, you know I do appreciate your help."

MAY 22, 1991 – "Bill, you are my friend, adopted brother, and lawyer. Do I need say more about where we stand with one another? . . . Please do not fret so."

SEPTEMBER 11, 1991 – "How is the best lawyer in the world doing these days?" (He wrote this greeting at least ten times.)

JANUARY 14, 1992 – "You are my best friend and attorney, and we are one in this to the end. . . . As I've told you before, I trust you and know you have my best interest at heart."

APRIL 3, 1992 – "Just think, Monday, April 6, we will have known each other five years. May it last another fifty years or so."

APRIL 5, 1993 – "Tomorrow is our six-year anniversary. 'Happy Anniversary.' Please don't go getting the seven-year itch on me. Time sure does fly by fast when you are having fun."

NOVEMBER 7, 1993 – "How's the best lawyer and friend in the world doing on this lovely fall evening we are having in this area?"

JUNE 29, 2003 – "I see every day on the local news people who really need a good lawyer. Are you catching any of those cases?"

SEPTEMBER 15, 2003 – "I talked for a moment with one of your clients on Friday, Danny Aria. He was up to the ID department. He said he had you for a lawyer. He sure needs one. . . . I told him he had a good lawyer." (I didn't become his lawyer until after his trial was over and he had his sentences. I told Donald that I was trying to correct the situation.)

MARCH 11, 2004 – "I do believe Martha Stewart should have had you for a lawyer. She should have taken the deal."

JUNE 25, 2004 – "How's the best lawyer in the USA and the world? . . . Don't get a big head for all the praises I've given you."

18. Confession

As I approached the courthouse at seven o'clock the following morning, my experience of twelve years working in the prosecutor's office came back to me. In the past I had often entered that building early in the morning, but if the door was locked I always had a key. Now I could envision myself beating on the door until eight o'clock.

At the door, I knocked loudly, and within seconds Hank Dresher, one of the investigators, opened the door. He had been waiting for me and directed me to the grand jury room. As I passed the security door leading to the offices, the door was open. Beyond the long corridor, lined with caverns, I could see the back door. The door had just opened, and my handcuffed client entered, escorted by a deputy sheriff. I waved, but Harvey could only nod his head.

Two tables had been set up near the entrance to the grand jury room. Two homicide investigators, Jim Lawson and Ron Camden, sat on one side of one of the tables. Camden was dressed rather formally in a dark suit and dark tie. Lawson was more informal, wearing a gray-green sport coat and tan slacks. I thought their dress reflected their personalities.

Two empty chairs faced them. I was directed to one of the empty seats. Harvey entered and was directed to the other. Even though he wore dark blue prison garb, Harvey looked neat and well dressed. He was clean shaven. His handcuffs were removed, and he was instructed not to leave the chair without permission.

I observed that a video camera was mounted on a tripod, its eye directed at Harvey, and incidentally at me.

Harvey was smiling and upbeat. He greeted me and the two investigators and was introduced to everyone else. Terry Gaines and Joe Deters were seated against the wall behind us at the other table. Gaines was dressed in a wrinkled light tan summer suit. Deters's black suit and black-and-white tie were appropriate for a funeral. After that initial introduction, Harvey seemed to forget Gaines and Deters. The room was filled with activity. Wires snaked across the table.

Ron Camden asked me to step outside the room. Once there he questioned me, "You told Ney and Vollman that there was evidence of Harvey's actions ready at hand?"

I nodded.

"What is it?"

"Donald Harvey was systematically poisoning Carl Hoeweler with arsenic for four years. His hair and nails have to be loaded with it."

Camden's eyes went blank, and expression left his face. I could almost see the wheels turning in his head. His eyes focused on me again. "We would have found that."

"If you had known to look. He was down here for interviews at least twice." I smiled, and we returned to the grand jury room.

As the preparations were continuing, I was informed that Ney and others were in his office and there was a radio transmission to them. During a break in the questioning later that day, I had an occasion to go to Ney's office, where I found the room filled. Ney and Vollman were there, along with Frank Cleveland, the Hamilton County coroner, with one of his assistants, and Lt. Bill Fletcher, commander of the Cincinnati Homicide/Rape Squad, with one of his assistants.

Later, when I told Minarcin of the radio transmission between offices, he was incredulous, saying that anyone knowing the frequency or finding the frequency accidentally could have tuned in to the entire confession.

Before the session started, Ron Camden said he wanted a cup of coffee. Harvey spoke up, "I guess you wouldn't want me to fix it for you." Nervous laughter rippled through the room as Camden declined the offer and went to get his own coffee.

The session began at 7:21 A.M. with an opening statement by Deters. He announced that the purpose of the meeting was to take a deposition from

Donald Harvey pursuant to the signed agreement between Harvey and the prosecutor's office. He administered an oath to Harvey. I thought this ludicrous. According to the plea bargain, if Harvey lied at this time he would be facing the electric chair. He could hardly be concerned about the possibility of being charged with perjury. But the action was innocuous, so I kept silent. Deters directed the officers to read Harvey his rights. Lawson did so, and Harvey acknowledged his understanding.

I had to be there, but I felt like a fifth wheel. My presence was really more important to the prosecutors than it was to my client. I had instructed Donald, and I knew he would cooperate. He didn't need my protection from questions he didn't want to answer. He had to answer. His fate had already been decided. But the prosecutors were determined to do everything by the book. They wouldn't risk anything that might be challenged in court. So it was important for Harvey to have legal representation.

Lawson led the questioning, primarily with open-ended questions. Camden occasionally interjected more specific questions to elicit details.

Harvey appeared to be alert, calm, and affable. Throughout the lengthy interview he showed less emotion than a subordinate might in a performance appraisal, with occasional flashes of humor. He had before him the handwritten document he had prepared at my direction, and he referred to it each time he started to talk about another death. Upon questioning, he affirmed that he had produced the list solely from his own memory, without any assistance. He apologized for not remembering specific dates and said that the deaths of some of the patients might be out of order.

He avoided using the word murder, apparently preferring euphemisms. His favorite was "took care of." Several times when he used this expression, one of the questioners would inquire whether he was speaking of providing care for someone in the course of his duties or causing the patient's death.

He told about causing the deaths of Nathaniel Watson, Leon Nelson, and Virgil Weddle. He did not mention Doris Nally, who was not on his list. She had somehow slipped his mind.

Harvey told about killing Edward Schreibeis. He wasn't sure whether his next victim was Robert Crockett or Henry Cody, but he remembered the details. (Crockett was correct.) His report on that death was interrupted by a need to change the tape, and the group took a short break. Harvey was permitted to go to the bathroom.

Asked how he chose between arsenic and cyanide, Harvey said that he preferred arsenic because of the odor of the cyanide.

Harvey confused the order of the next few deaths. He gave accounts of the deaths of Ernest Frey and Donald Barney. Following another short break, he apologized for not knowing the answers to all of the detectives' questions and explained that he had tried to forget. He told about killing James Woods.

He explained that the reason he caused deaths mostly of men was that most of his patients were men. He said that the women were in better shape. He was grateful that his father had died suddenly and didn't suffer, because extended life in a poor condition was hard on the family.

Harvey returned to his confession, reporting on the death of Clayborn Kendrick. After another break, he told about Roger Evans. He accepted a cup of coffee and went on to talk about Milton Canter and Mose Thompson.

Lawson told him that he could have a break whenever he was tired. He acknowledged the offer but continued. He told about killing Bill Collins, Albert Buehlmann, Odas Day, and Cleo Fish. He skipped Cody. He told about his unsuccessful attempts to poison John Oldendick and Harold White and talked about patients he considered as candidates and decided against.

He told about killing Leo Parker, Margaret Kuckro, and Stella Lemon. He skipped over John Powell, saying that he had already testified about him for eight hours. He reported on Hilda Leitz and Joseph Pike.

Harvey said he had nothing to do with the death of Ruth Gillispie. When asked why he volunteered that information, he replied that he had heard her name mentioned, and he just wanted to keep the record straight.

At this point, the questioners took a break for dinner. Harvey was hand-cuffed to be returned to his cell. My first thought was for the safety of my client. I feared that after he was returned to the jail by one of the investigators from the prosecutor's office, the other inmates would realize that he was coop-erating with the prosecutor and might take some retaliatory action against him. My fears were relieved when I saw that Hank Dresher was taking charge of Harvey. I had known Dresher for fifteen years and had confidence in him.

Tired and hungry, I walked to Diane's Restaurant, half a block from the courthouse, feeling very much alone. Harvey and I had been opposed by a large group, both in the room with them and listening in Ney's office via radio transmission. I supposed that the prosecution team would have piled into a couple of the county cars to head for some fine restaurant.

Looking out through the larger plate-glass windows of the restaurant, I was surprised to see the group coming to Diane's. They gathered around my table and joined me for dinner. The subject of Donald's confession could not be avoided.

The deputy coroner was seated next to me, and I took the opportunity to ask what he thought of Harvey's account. He said that the account was credible. In response to questions from Gaines, he indicated that Harvey's information about the properties of cyanide and arsenic was correct.

I was able to keep a calm exterior and convey the impression that I believed my client, but I recognized the possibility that Harvey had fabricated the whole story for some reason of his own. Some time later I learned that the prosecutors had disbelieved him. Their strategy in agreeing to the plea bargain and confession was to gain the information they needed to disprove his story. I am certain that their objective at that point was to discredit Pat Minarcin.

In a fairly typical reaction to the grim way in which they had spent their day, the group was jovial. They resorted to black humor to counteract their emotional involvement. Some pretended to be checking their food for tampering, and no one ordered pudding.

I observed that on this occasion, as throughout my experiences with Harvey, people found it incomprehensible that a man who admitted to being responsible for so many deaths could be so warm and friendly and have such a quick sense of humor.

When the interrogation was resumed after the break for dinner, Harvey said that he was responsible for one more death at Drake, but he couldn't remember the man's name. He remembered the circumstances. In response to a direct question, he said that this could possibly be Henry Cody.

The detectives read a list of names and asked Harvey if he recognized any of them. Some he identified as having been patients on his ward, and some he said he had provided care for. One he said he had autopsied. He denied that any of them were his victims. He used the word "victim" reluctantly.

Harvey had confessed to being responsible for twenty-three deaths at Drake Hospital.

At this point, the detectives made a distinct shift in the questioning to ask about deaths in Hamilton County outside Drake Hospital. First, Lawson asked who was the first person in Hamilton County whose death he caused. Harvey replied that he did not know, but it happened at the VA hospital. The detectives agreed that the VA hospital would be excluded from the questioning at this time.

Harvey asked for a break to confer with me. He wanted to verify that he should tell them about deaths he caused outside the hospital. I told him that was part of the plea bargain. When he was ready to resume, he said that he would prefer to start with the most recent, because he was having trouble remembering. He confessed to the murders of Edward Wilson, Helen Metzger, Henry Hoeweler, and James Peluso. He confessed to giving less than fatal doses of poison to Carl Hoeweler, Diane Alexander, and Margaret Hoeweler. He admitted giving serum from both hepatitis and AIDS patients to Diane Alexander. He also described the accidental poisoning of Howard Vetter. He told about the incident of food poisoning of guests at Carl's holiday party for his staff.

Questioned further about administration of poison to Carl Hoeweler, Harvey told of giving him small doses of arsenic over a three-year period. He said he never gave cyanide to Carl.

The detectives then asked him about the VA hospital. Harvey related the story of his discharge, or forced resignation. He said that his ambition had been to become supervisor of the morgue, and just as he had achieved that goal, it was unfairly taken away from him. He pointed out that he had received three superior performance awards and two other awards from the hospital.

Asked about deaths he had caused at the VA hospital, he replied that he couldn't remember. He reminded the detectives that a lot of time had passed and that he was in a turbulent period of his life when he started there. Prompted, he said that he could remember two. He told about accidentally causing the death of Hiram Proffit through an overdose of heparin when working in the heart catheterization laboratory. He described smothering a patient, whom he identified incorrectly as a Mr. Gant, with a pillow on February 12, 1978. He remembered the date because it was his last day before being transferred to work in the morgue. The man was in critical condition. Harvey was fond of him and wanted to "take care of him" before he left.

Pressed for further names, Harvey said that he could remember no more. Conscious of the importance of a complete confession, I asked whether he thought he could remember the names if the officers presented him with a list of patients he might have killed. Harvey said it was possible that he would be able to. Asked for a number, he indicated there were ten to fifteen. He said that any deaths he had caused were by disconnecting the breathing apparatus, putting air bubbles into veins, or smothering. He said he used no poisons at the VA hospital. The officers indicated that they would attempt to obtain such a list.

The officers led him through a recounting of his work experience from the time he left the Air Force. He repeatedly denied that he had caused any deaths at any other hospitals. Nobody mentioned Marymount. I would have jumped in immediately to say Kentucky was off limits, but it wasn't necessary. Donald was very good about following my instructions.

Asked about his interest in working in the morgue, Donald said that he liked finding out the causes of death. He acknowledged that he enjoyed finding that doctors and nurses had made errors, especially faulty diagnoses. He denied that he had caused any deaths with the goal of fooling the medical professionals.

Donald stated that every patient he gave arsenic or cyanide at Drake Hospital had been diagnosed as being in terminal condition and had been sent there to die. I thought Camden might challenge that to weaken the "mercy killing" argument, but he let it stand. Of course we all knew that Donald's sentence had already been established, so the detectives and the prosecutors had no incentive to deal with motive. And I couldn't blame Donald for trying to put a better face on his acts of murder.

The detectives inquired about the reading materials found in his trailer. After kidding them about looking at his "dirty books," he said that he had many books on eastern religions because he was interested in religion. He said he had been baptized a Catholic and had joined the Mormon Church. He said he had acquired many of the books in used condition and had not read all of them.

When asked about satanic services, he said that he had never attended such a service with others—that he had conducted such services alone. Pushed on this point, he declared that he had belonged to a group in Kentucky, but while it was occult, it was not satanic. He didn't mention his induction into the coven in North Carolina. I let that go, because it wasn't pertinent to the plea bargain.

He said he had never taken human body parts or used any in a service, nor had he used blood. He said he wouldn't use blood, because he was afraid of AIDS. He told them that although he had heard about sacrifice of chickens or other animals in voodoo services, he had never been involved in voodoo.

He acknowledged that he had an altar set up on his dresser when he lived with Carl, and that Carl knew about it. He insisted that Carl, however, was never involved in his occult practices. Asked to describe one of his services, he refused. I was prepared to support his refusal, but the detectives did not pursue that line of questioning.

The interview had been going on for approximately twelve hours, and the principals were noticeably tired. Donald looked fresher than any of the others. In some perverse way, he seemed to be enjoying himself. A psychologist might have concluded that he felt relief that he was finally unloading these gruesome secrets. I think it was more likely that he was reveling in the attention. The session was ended at this point.

The questioning was resumed a week later in the same room. Harvey looked almost jaunty in a long-sleeved sweatshirt under his blue prison outfit. He was again sworn in and read his rights. He acknowledged that he was on no medication at that time and that he was participating willingly. He was reminded that he could refuse to answer any question, that he could pause at any time to consult me, and that he could ask for a break whenever he wanted one. The prosecutors were taking no chances on procedures.

Harvey was apparently relaxed and cooperative, but this interview was much less productive than the one a week earlier. Harvey appeared to be poorly organized. The primary topic was deaths at the VA hospital, and Harvey pointed out that he was being asked to remember events that were ten years in the past. He was confused about dates and frequently corrected himself. He often said, "I can't remember," or made contradictory statements. He could remember room numbers, but not names.

During the interview, there was a pause while Camden changed the batteries in the radio transmitter. He had difficulty remembering the way they went in, and Harvey quipped, "You can't remember something for five minutes and you expect me to remember things that happened ten years ago." Camden didn't seem to think that was funny.

Lawson showed Harvey a list of patients who had died at the VA hospital during the time he worked as a nursing assistant. Harvey studied it at length, making some pencil marks on the list.

"Did you do anything to any of these people to cause their death?"
"Yes."
"How many?"
After some thought, Harvey answered, "Six."
Asked for details, Harvey repeatedly said, "I know I was in his room, and when I left he was dead, but I don't know anything I did to kill him."

He finally concluded that the patient he had referred to as Mr. Gant in the previous interview was actually Sterling Moore. He was definite about causing the death of Joseph C. Harris by reducing his oxygen supply. He indicated that he thought he was responsible for the deaths of James A. Twitty, James R. Ritter, and Harry Rhodes, but he could supply no corroborating details. Asked about the marks he had put on the list, he said that he checked names he recognized, but that he didn't know what, if anything, he had done to them.

Donald Harvey is led by guards to his trial.

(above) Two-year-old Donald in 1954.
(below) The Harvey home where Donald was raised in Booneville, Kentucky.

Goldie and Ray Harvey, Donald's parents, in 1979

(above) A grade-school photo of Donald, approximately nine years old.
(below) Donald, at seven.

(above) Donald at a family Christmas party in 1985.
(below) Donald beams with pride after buying his first home.

The court proceedings, including a chart with the names of victims.

(above) Pat Minarcin, who broke the case while the news anchor of WCPO-TV.

(above) Donald in 1992, serving his life sentence.
(below) The Warren County [Ohio] Correctional Facility where Donald lives.

19. Forensic Experts

Hamilton County Prosecutor Art Ney had a confession, but he had a problem. He didn't know what to believe. He knew that a confession without corroboration was insufficient. Every prosecutor is familiar with the phenomenon of a false confession. The plea bargain I had negotiated for Donald Harvey would close the case satisfactorily only if Harvey's confession were accurate and complete, covering all the deaths Harvey had caused in Hamilton County. Harvey had his incentive to make the list complete; he would gain no immunity for cases discovered after indictment and sentencing. But he could well have reasons for confessing to deaths he had not caused.

I knew Donald quite well by then; we had spent a lot of time together. He had shown me the complexity of his personality. He had demonstrated a sense of humor and, as reluctant as I was to recognize it, charm. He seemed quite ready to tell people what he thought they wanted to hear, whether true or not. He had fabricated some outrageous stories in talking to me and had glib explanations when confronted with their impossibility. I think he could even deceive himself into believing his own lies. I knew he was beginning to enjoy his notoriety. I didn't know how much of his confession was true.

Corroboration was hard to obtain. The bodies had been cremated or buried. There had been few autopsies. Witnesses' recollections were not likely to be sharp regarding circumstances surrounding deaths on a floor where ninety-five percent of the patients were not expected to leave the hospital alive. Hospital records were terse. Hospital officials were uncooperative.

Ney decided to enlist expert assistance. He and Assistant Prosecutor Joe Deters flew to Richmond, Virginia, to take a deposition from Dr. Robert V. Blanke, forensic toxicologist at the Clinical Support Center, Medical College of Virginia, Virginia Commonwealth University.

Dr. Blanke's specialty was stability of drugs in tissues. He was professor emeritus of Virginia Commonwealth University. He held a Ph.D. in pharmacology from the Illinois University School of Medicine and was certified by the American Board of Forensic Toxicology. He was a past president of the Society of Forensic Toxicologists and a founding member of the American Academy of Forensic Toxicologists. He had a hundred publications in the field. In his career, he had been chief toxicologist of the Illinois State Health Department and chief toxicologist of the Virginia Medical Examiner's Office. He had been qualified as an expert witness in many states, including Ohio.

They videotaped the interview. Dr. Blanke's appearance was perfectly suited to establishing his credibility as an expert. Seated at a table in an impressive office, he wore a white laboratory coat. His white hair and glasses completed the picture of a trusted medical advisor.

Ney, wearing his customary tan coat and black tie, offered a prologue for the benefit of the recording, stating the purpose of the visit. He said that he had offered me the opportunity to be present when they took the deposition, and I had declined. I didn't see that Donald had any interests to be protected in the deposition by Blanke.

I noted with amusement when I viewed the videotape that Joe Deters was again dressed as for a funeral.

Ney first asked Dr. Blanke to talk about cyanide. Dr. Blanke said that when people use the term "cyanide," they may be referring to hydrogen cyanide, a deadly gas, or to cyanide salts, either sodium cyanide or potassium cyanide. The latter are white crystalline compounds that dissolve easily in water.

Cyanide poisons enzymes and causes anoxic death in a matter of minutes, even seconds if cyanide gas is inhaled or the salts are injected into the bloodstream. Cyanide death is slightly slower if the poison is ingested, but is still rapid, perhaps ten to twenty minutes.

Cyanides hydrolyze in the body to form hydrogen cyanide, which has a distinctive odor that persists for several days. Not everyone can smell it (see chapter 3). Because hydrogen cyanide is acid, it causes an irritation of the stomach lining, which might be noticed by a pathologist, although many other acidic substances could be responsible for such an inflammation.

Embalming fluids contain formaldehyde along with phenols, perfumes, dyes, and other ingredients. If cyanide is present, it reacts with the formaldehyde and is destroyed. Pathologists could not definitely conclude that cyanide was the cause of death if an autopsy were performed after embalming.

If a body were not embalmed, cyanide could be detected if decomposition had not proceeded too far. The pathologist could look for cyanide derivatives. An unrefrigerated body would probably decompose in two or three days to the point that ordinary procedures would not show evidence of cyanide. Very sophisticated tests of brain tissue, vitreous humor, or spinal fluid might indicate the presence of cyanide up to a year later, but the evidence would not be conclusive. The forensic determination is complicated by the fact that a trace of cyanide is produced by the normal process of decomposition.

Ney then asked about arsenic. Arsenic is an easy poison to detect. It is permanent in the body. All people have some arsenic in their systems; the quantity is the key to pathological examination. As little as an eighth of a teaspoon (150 to 200 milligrams) could be fatal, but tolerance varies widely. Small doses administered over time would make a person sick, causing nausea, vomiting, and diarrhea. Such an illness is very difficult to diagnose, since a virus could cause the same symptoms. Arsenic is cumulative in the system. It has an affinity for the proteins in hair and nails, so it is concentrated in those locations.

Strychnine is essentially indestructible and can be detected after embalming and after decomposition, Dr. Blanke said in response to a question. I don't know why Ney asked about strychnine. Donald had never mentioned that poison in his confession.

Cremation destroys organic poisons such as cyanide. Arsenic is not destroyed, but might be volatilized by the heat.

Dr. Blanke said that detection of other poisonous materials, such as adhesive cleaner or rat poison, would depend upon the specific compositions, and he could not comment on those without further information. He added that rat poison would probably not be fatal to humans. Warfarin, the major ingredient in some rat poisons, would cause hemorrhaging and would be identifiable, even in embalmed tissue.

He pointed out that in an autopsy the pathologist examines all major organs to look for anything that is inconsistent with the diagnosis.

Deters showed Dr. Blanke the death certificates for patients named in Harvey's confession and asked his opinions as a forensic toxicologist, including whether there would be any merit in disinterring the bodies for forensic examination. Dr. Blanke's comments were:

Robert Crockett: *Symptoms could be consistent with cyanide poisoning. Exhumation unlikely to be informative.*

Ernest Charles Frey: *Symptoms not consistent with cyanide poisoning. No cyanide was detected in tissues from autopsy, but they had been preserved in formaldehyde. Could test the preserved tissues for arsenic. Exhumation unlikely to be informative.*

Donald Barney: *Symptoms consistent with cyanide, although no cyanide was detected in autopsy. Detection upon exhumation possible because Harvey said that he injected cyanide into Barney's buttock, which is muscle tissue. Muscle tissue would receive less embalming fluid than most organs and thus the cyanide might persist. He said the tissue around the injection site could be excised and tested for cyanide.*

James Woods: *Symptoms do not sound like cyanide death because he died later in another hospital. Exhumation unlikely to be informative.*

Clayborn Kendrick: *Symptoms too vague to evaluate. Exhumation unlikely to be informative.*

Roger Evans: *Symptoms indicate could be cyanide. Exhumation unlikely to be informative.*

Milton Canter: *Symptoms consistent with cyanide. Exhumation unlikely to be informative.*

Mose Thompson Jr.: *Symptoms consistent with cyanide. Exhumation unlikely to be informative.*

William Collins: *Symptoms consistent with cyanide. Exhumation unlikely to be informative.*

Dr. Blanke volunteered that there would be no reason for a clinician to be suspicious of these deaths. Deters continued with his presentation of death certificates for review.

Albert Buehlmann: *Symptoms do not sound like cyanide death. Exhumation unlikely to be informative.*

Odas Day: *Symptoms could indicate cyanide death. Exhumation unlikely to be informative.*

Cleo Fish: *Symptoms indicate could be cyanide. Exhumation unlikely to be informative.*

Leo Parker: *Because of the long time interval between dosage and death, cyanide not likely to be the actual cause of his death, although cyanide could have further weakened him and thus hastened his death. Parker was cremated, so no exhumation possible.*

Margaret Kuckro: *Symptoms are consistent with cyanide. Exhumation unlikely to be informative, but cyanide could possibly be detected because her death was more recent.*

Stella Lemon: *Because she was transferred off the ward and died some weeks later, it is unlikely that she died of cyanide poisoning, but cyanide could have worsened her condition. Exhumation unlikely to be informative.*

Henry Cody: *Symptoms are too vague for forming an opinion. Chances of obtaining useful information upon exhumation are nil.*

Dr. Blanke added that hospital deaths by poisoning generally involve multiple victims. He said that it would be difficult to identify any single death as murder. He said that a review panel at the hospital is the proper procedure.

Art Ney wanted a second expert opinion from a forensic pathologist regarding deaths other than by poisoning. He and Joe Deters flew to Detroit to take a deposition from Dr. Werner Spitz. Dr. Spitz's field of special expertise was death by asphyxiation. Dr. Spitz was an M.D., board certified in both anatomic and forensic pathology. He was chief medical examiner of Wayne County and a professor at Wayne State University. He had published seventy-seven scientific papers and a textbook on medico-legal investigation of death. He was on the editorial boards of the *Journal of the American Academy of Forensic Scientists* and the *Journal of the National Association of Medical Examiners*. He had frequently testified as an expert witness, including testimony in congressional investigations of the deaths of John F. Kennedy and Dr. Martin Luther King Jr. He had also been a consultant regarding deaths in the children's department of a large hospital.

This interview was also videotaped. Although Dr. Spitz's appearance was quite unlike that of Dr. Blanke, he also radiated an aura of authority. He had gray hair and bushy black eyebrows and a deeply furrowed forehead. His deliberate, precise speech in a middle-European accent projected scientific competence.

Dr. Spitz said that isolated incidences of killings of patients in hospitals are rare. In almost all cases in which a hospital staff member has intentionally caused the death of one patient, that person is guilty of multiple deaths. He recommended that hospitals routinely conduct autopsies and convene physician panels to review deaths. He said that the proper authorities should be notified immediately if any deaths appear suspicious.

He doesn't credit mercy killings.

He was asked to comment on deaths by suffocation. He responded that an autopsy is unlikely to show the cause of death if a terminally ill patient dies from suffocation. The findings of the autopsy are likely to be consistent with death from natural causes associated with the illness or injury that had resulted in hospitalization. Only external evidence, confession, or a witness would disclose the immediate cause of death. Pulling the plug on a respirator is not detectable in an autopsy.

Dr. Spitz said that injecting air into a vein would cause practically instantaneous death. An ordinary autopsy would not reveal the cause of death. It would be found only if the pathologist suspected an air embolism and conducted the autopsy underwater, which is almost never done. Exhumation would not reveal suffocation by injection of air.

In summary, Dr. Spitz said that there was plenty of evidence to conclude that there was more than one case—that a large number of deaths were involved. Harvey would have learned how to kill from his eighteen years of experience in hospitals. Dr. Spitz said that the methods of suffocation Harvey confessed he had used—a pillow, a plastic sheet, disconnecting apparatus, or injection of air into a vein—would not ordinarily be detectable in an autopsy and would not show up in an exhumed body. He felt there would be no merit in exhumation.

When I viewed this videotape, I wondered why Ney was so interested in deaths by deprivation of oxygen. Presumably he was following up on the deaths at the VA hospital, although Donald's confession had been vague about those deaths. It would have made a lot more sense for Handy to have pursued that method, but Ney had no knowledge of Donald's activities there.

Dr. Spitz also stated that autopsies yield only positive findings, not negative findings. They might verify some of Donald's claims, but they couldn't disprove them.

20. Forensic Psychiatry

The prosecutors needed to know. Was Donald Harvey competent to stand trial? Could his confession be believed? Would an insanity defense stand up in court? Although the insanity issue had been settled when the charge was a single murder, that of John Powell, Harvey's confession to multiple murders raised the question anew. Wouldn't he have to be crazy to kill more than thirty people, many of them practically strangers?

I wasn't considering an insanity defense. Donald didn't want it. He was reconciled to sixty years in prison according to the plea bargain. Neither he nor I wanted to risk upsetting the agreement.

But Art Ney was taking no chances. He wanted consultation with another expert. He assigned this deposition to Joe Deters.

Deters sought help from Emanuel Tanay, M.D., a specialist in forensic psychiatry. Dr. Tanay was a professor of psychiatry at the College of Medicine at Wayne State University. He had written a book on homicide. Among his more famous cases had been Jack Ruby and Ted Bundy. Deters requested Dr. Tanay to examine Harvey.

Dr. Tanay was thorough. He watched the videotapes of Harvey's confession. He reviewed the clinical reports and discussed the case with Deters. Dr. Blanke also called him about the case. Only then did he interview Harvey.

The interview lasted about two hours. Dr. Tanay began by introducing himself and overtly starting a tape recorder. He stressed that he was conducting the interview at the request of the prosecutor and that the interview was not confidential; he would provide a report to the prosecutor. He was not Donald's doctor. This interview was not an interrogation, and I was not present. Attorneys are not usually included in psychiatric interviews, because the examiners consider our presence counterproductive for the purpose of the interviews. Since this interview followed Donald's confession, he really had no interests for me to protect. I had no basis for telling Donald not to answer any questions, so long as they were confined to deaths in Hamilton County. I was provided with a tape of the interview.

When Harvey had indicated his understanding and agreement, Dr. Tanay asked him for a biographical sketch. Harvey told him about his early life and his family and about his service in the Air Force.

That led to a discussion of Harvey's homosexuality, a recurring theme throughout the interview. Harvey told Dr. Tanay of his suicide attempts and his psychiatric counseling. He said that the counseling was because of his depression and attempts at suicide, not because of his homosexuality.

When they moved on to talking about Harvey's work in hospitals, Dr. Tanay introduced the subject of causing death. "Tell me, when did you first get the idea about inducing death in someone?"

"I can talk from Cincinnati on. I cannot talk about when I worked at other hospitals [in the] past."

"Prior, that would be because of the immunity problem."

"Immunity problem, yes. I can only talk . . ."

"I can understand that, but, you know, let's not be specific so there would be no problem of any type of legal consequences. Okay. So let's not be specific. But you know you cannot be charged with anything that is not specific. At least that's my view. I'm not a lawyer so don't take legal advice from me."

"Okay. I'll talk . . ."

With some difficulty, Dr. Tanay and Harvey worked out a way to talk about what Dr. Tanay wanted to know. Harvey would mention no places and avoid use of names relative to any deaths outside Hamilton County. I would not have been comfortable with that process and would have advised Donald to continue to refuse to talk about Marymount. This interview was taking place before we had a signed plea agreement with Handy. Fortunately, this premature discussion did not compromise that plea bargain.

Dr. Tanay was able to return to his question of getting the idea of inducing a death. "What seems to give rise to it?"

"I guess the helplessness of the individual."

"Does it come impulsively or does it...?"

"It's like there's another individual. Like sometimes I have control of it, sometimes I don't. . . . I was always a timid person. But when I've done this, it's always like I've been very domineering, very well in control of my emotions."

Harvey went on to describe how he gathered information about a patient and made a decision to induce a death. When I studied the transcript of this interview, I was amused by the recurrent use of the phrase "induce a death." It was Dr. Tanay's euphemism, and it seemed to work with Donald. Dr. Tanay probed for Donald's feelings after causing a death. Donald answered, "I felt it was right. I never felt I was wrong."

"You were right because of what?"

"When a person says, 'Please let me die, help me die, do something for me,' and this goes on for days and days, then it would be time to make my decision to, uh, induce death."

Dr. Tanay didn't question at that point Donald's implication that he killed only patients who had asked to die. He discussed some of the specific cases with Donald and then turned to the period during which Donald worked in the morgue at the VA hospital. During that time, Donald caused no deaths of patients. When Dr. Tanay asked why he had killed no one during that time, Donald's quick answer was that he had no access to patients.

Upon further questioning, Donald said that he was happy with his work and his other involvements. Dr. Tanay seized on that response. "So there was no need to."

"No."

Dr. Tanay resumed asking about individual cases to which Donald had confessed, inquiring about his feelings. Donald repeatedly used the term "relieved." Dr. Tanay asked about that. "What is there that is a relief about death?"

"Well, if I had my chance and knew that I could die, if someone would shoot me right here in the heart, then it would be over for me. I would not—it'd just be—it's a nice, peaceful feeling. They're out of their misery."

"Why didn't you take arsenic yourself?"

"I don't know. I had cyanide, too. Why not take cyanide?"

"Yes, why not?"

"I think one reason is because I want my story told—not for the glory, not for the glamour, just my story told—that if there is people [sic] out there that is doing this, then they should be stopped. Maybe it will stop one person."

Donald initiated talking about his interest in the occult, but Dr. Tanay did not pursue that angle. He returned to individual cases. He asked intensively about Donald's thoughts about what he termed mercy killings. They also talked at length about Donald's relationships with Carl and Diane.

Dr. Tanay inquired about Donald's perceptions of his arrest and his expectations with regard to his trial. They discussed the possibility of an insanity defense. Donald talked at length and with strong feelings about his innocence with regard to some things he was accused of doing, especially with regard to his firing from the VA hospital, while not denying his responsibility for the deaths he caused.

Dr. Tanay returned to the central issue of the interview. "Well, you know, we're not any closer to an understanding of why you would kill these people at the hospital."

"I felt it was, uh, to put them out of their misery."

"You know, let me tell you, that is not my understanding. You know, I have encountered a lot of people that have engaged in what you would call mercy killings. You did not, in my opinion. You use that as an excuse, as a camouflage. I believe that you had a need to induce death and it makes it less difficult, more acceptable, to do it with people who are sick than with people who are well—for example, one impression I have, for whatever it is worth, is that somehow the passiveness, the sickness, made you very angry. You identified with them. You didn't like for them to be in that state. Like, for example, one of the cases you related to me was somebody who may have recovered, and yet you couldn't tolerate his state of being in this type of a passive state, and you right away had to become active and then you felt better, relieved. Do you follow me?"

"Yeah, I'm following you."

"This is a kind of thought that I have and I wonder if it rings any bells in your mind."

"Well, like I said, you know, sometimes I would feel real depressed before this would happen, or . . ."

"So that, in a way, doing it would . . ."

"Relieved the depression that I felt. I felt relief that they were out of their misery, but I also felt relief for myself, too."

"For yourself, yes."

When Donald returned to saying that he was putting them out of their misery, Dr. Tanay disagreed. "No, to end your misery. There is, somehow, your misery in there and you have to do it."

It seemed to me that Dr. Tanay departed from the purpose of his interview. I supposed he couldn't resist his own urge to treat Donald. But he had gathered the data he needed for his report to Deters.

Following Dr. Tanay's interview with Donald Harvey, Deters took Dr. Tanay's videotaped deposition for presentation to the grand jury. Dr. Tanay, seated behind a desk, wearing a tan suit and a striped tie, seemed like a professor lecturing to a small group of graduate students. Carl Vollman and Terry Gaines from the prosecutor's office were also present.

Dr. Tanay was well organized. He said that state of mind is a legal issue. He gave a brief discourse on psychiatric theory.

Dr. Tanay emphasized that a personality disorder is a structural problem, not a mental illness. He said that a personality disorder may be useful to the individual, citing the example that a compulsive personality could be helpful to a tax accountant.

Speaking specifically about the interview, Dr. Tanay summarized his findings:

> *Donald Harvey was the product of a difficult childhood. His mother was only sixteen [sic] years old and unprepared for motherhood. His father was seldom at home. Donald felt neglected. He was a victim of homosexual pedophilia, being sexually abused by an uncle who was eleven [sic] years older.*

> *Harvey considers himself to be homosexual. He had two heterosexual experiences in his life, both while intoxicated. He has had over four hundred [sic] homosexual encounters.*

> *Harvey caused deaths before coming to Ohio, but no details were given. He engaged in no homicidal activity when he worked as a diener in the morgue.*

> *Harvey kept records of the deaths he caused and remembers them well. The deaths brought him relief.*

> *Harvey is an intelligent individual. He makes good choices for his morbid satisfactions.*

Harvey is a compulsive killer. He does not have a conscience.

He had a choice and knows the wrongfulness of his acts. He avoided detection for a long time.

Harvey's motivation to confess was confrontation with the incriminating evidence.

Dr. Tanay stated his opinions of the legal issues as a forensic psychiatrist:

Harvey is telling the truth, although some details may be inaccurate.

Harvey was sane at the time of the acts of which he is charged. Harvey is competent to stand trial.

Harvey's claim that the deaths he induced were mercy killings is not credible.

There is a likelihood that Harvey would continue to attempt to kill in jail if given the opportunity.

21. A Second Opinion

Donald Harvey was also interviewed by Walter W. Lippert, Ph.D., a clinical psychologist who often worked for the Hamilton County prosecutors.

Dr. Lippert interviewed Harvey for four and a half hours. His report confirmed Tanay's major findings and provided additional insight into Donald Harvey's motivations and behavior.

As had Dr. Tanay, Dr. Lippert had Harvey tell him about his childhood, including his early induction into homosexual behavior. Dr. Lippert explored the deaths at Marymount in more depth than Dr. Tanay had. As this interview took place after we had a plea bargain with Handy, I removed my instruction to Donald to refuse to talk about Marymount.

Dr. Lippert inquired about Harvey's interpersonal relationships throughout his life. He asked Harvey for his own explanations of why he had induced the deaths and for his feelings about what he had done.

In his report, Dr. Lippert based his analysis of Harvey on a generally accepted list of distinguishing psychopathic traits as described by Hervey Cleckley, M.D., in a book entitled *Mask of Sanity*. He concluded that these traits accurately described Donald Harvey as having a psychopathic-type personality disorder.

Number one on Dr. Cleckley's list was superficial charm and good intelligence. Dr. Lippert observed that this description fit Donald Harvey exactly. Throughout their interview and in his personal history, Harvey exhibited a pleasant and engaging manner. His intelligence was intact, and he showed no obvious delusions or illusions.

Second on the list was absence of nervousness or secondary neurotic manifestations. Harvey was calm during the interview, maintaining eye contact, never shying away from making statements, and never displaying by body language any reticence or fear. These traits are not indicative of a psychopathic personality disorder, but are consistent with it.

More difficult to assess during an interview was unreliability, which had to be inferred from personal history. Dr. Lippert said that promises given with apparent sincerity were honored only if they met Harvey's needs.

Dr. Lippert was less inclined than Dr. Tanay to believe Harvey. He said that lying of a pathological nature is very typical and is to be expected. Truth and falsehood are not differentiated; either is used to further a goal.

A key trait was lack of remorse or shame. Donald told him that he had no regrets over what he had done. He felt no emotional pain for having caused pain for others. He found it easy to justify his behavior to himself by rationalization.

Another key trait was inadequately motivated antisocial behavior. The typical criminal usually has a goal of some gain, usually financial, and tries to minimize risk. With Harvey, on the other hand, the behavior itself, i.e., killing someone, appeared to be the goal. Harvey had nothing to gain. Furthermore, any efforts to avoid detection were more of an afterthought than part of a plan. His years of killing before he was suspected were the result of luck in choosing a pattern of murder that would not be readily apparent unless someone was looking for it. He chose victims because of their availability, but he aroused no suspicion because they were expected to die.

Dr. Lippert reported that Harvey also exhibited the key trait of poor judgment and failure to learn by experience. He usually acted on impulse with little regard for future consequences. The failure to learn from experience resulted in repeating the behavior of a destructive nature over and over again.

Harvey showed a pathological egocentricity and an incapacity for love. Dr. Lippert observed that Harvey had a tremendous need for control and viewed relationships with others only from his own point of view. When thwarted, he became angry and retaliatory. He lacked empathy or concern for others' welfare, using others to meet his needs.

Another distinguishing trait was poverty in major affective reactions. Observing that Harvey showed superficial gentleness and humor, Dr. Lippert concluded that this behavior was for theatrical effect and did not display inner feelings.

A related trait on Dr. Cleckley's list was specific lack of insight. Harvey knew the words and could talk about feelings and motivations, but in the absence of emotional content, he could not put any insight to use, and thus it was empty.

Harvey had many acquaintances and many brief sexual encounters, but he lacked the capacity to develop friendships of any depth. The interpersonal relationships were basically manipulative on his part and on the part of his companion of the moment. Each was concerned about meeting his own needs, and there was no basis of caring. His sex life was strictly for momentary pleasure, without emotional intimacy.

Harvey's attempts at suicide were typical of a person with psychopathic personality disorder. They stemmed from depression, but not depression caused by feelings of guilt. They were manipulative, undertaken in circumstances that would lead to rescue.

In typical behavior, Harvey followed no life plan. His frequent changes of employment, locations, religious affiliations, living arrangements, and companions reflected a basic aimlessness and responses to immediate impulses.

Dr. Lippert wrote to me:

"In summary, Donald Harvey presents as a psychopathic-type personality disorder. There are narcissistic traits about him, and thus there is a grandiose sense of self-importance, or preoccupation with his own power, [an exhibitionist who] wants constant attention and admiration, and a cool indifference to other people's hurts and pains. [Such people] are individuals who feel quite entitled to the special attention they receive, they're quite capable at any time to engage in interpersonal exploitativeness, taking advantage of others, to indulge in their own desires, and their relationships characteristically alternate between extreme over-idealization and devaluation. The most profound absence is that of empathy, the total inability to recognize how others feel, unable to appreciate the distress of someone who is seriously ill.

"They are not treatable by modern day psychological techniques. They are not experiencing an illness that would respond to chemotherapy; etiology is most probably genetic exacerbated by environmental disorder."

22. A Tricky Maneuver

My phone buzzed. The caller refused to identify himself. When I picked up the phone, the caller began, "Are you an attorney?"

"Yes."

"Are you the attorney for Donald Harvey?"

"Yes."

"Does Harvey have a bond?"

"Yes."

"Is he still incarcerated?"

"Yes."

"What is the bond?"

"Two hundred thousand dollars cash."

Without accent, the evenly modulated voice continued as the caller explained he was with the *New York Post* and said they were sending someone to Cincinnati to make Harvey's bond. The caller then asked me what time the clerk's office closed and whether the clerk would accept that much cash.

The conversation left me confused. There was only one reason to obtain Harvey's release. The newspaper would get an exclusive story, and then Harvey would be abandoned. I had an ethical dilemma. On the face of it, I would be acting against my client's interests if I thwarted an attempt to free him. But I was concerned for Harvey's welfare. If he were released, he had nowhere to go. He was unemployable, and he couldn't return to Carl's. I also feared that if Harvey were released, he might kill again. Dr. Tanay had said that he might kill again even in jail if he had the opportunity. I couldn't let that happen. So it wouldn't really be working against my client's interests to foil the attempt to free him on bond, because one more death would surely send him to the electric chair.

It was 10:00 A.M. Harvey would be out in public by 4:00 P.M. Now what should I do? When the bond was set, the court had not been concerned about the possibility that a serial killer might be released into the public. The bond had been set when the court believed that Harvey had killed only one person. With the revelations of additional deaths, no one had thought to raise the bond.

For half an hour, I debated. Not sure where to go or whom to talk to, I headed for the chambers of Judge William Mathews. I considered Mathews, the judge on the Harvey case, a friend.

My knock on the mahogany door invoked, "Come in." When I entered, the judge inquired, "What's up?"

Sitting on the edge of the red leather seat, I explained the phone call. Without hesitation, the judge picked up the phone and ordered someone to his office.

Within minutes, with a knock on the back door, Joe Deters entered. Judge Mathews asked me to repeat the story.

"Goddamn!" Deters exploded. "We can't let him out."

We discussed alternative courses of action, but all would expose me for leaking the news and perhaps violating my responsibility to protect my client's interests.

Once again the judge picked up his phone. He called Robert Jennings, the clerk of courts. The tall, lanky, slow-moving clerk was unflappable. He was loved and respected by almost everyone in the courthouse. Again, I explained the telephone call.

"Those bastards!" Silence held the room before Jennings snapped his fingers. "I've got it. Joe, file a motion to increase the bond. Judge, can we have a hearing at two?"

"Sure."

"Good." The clerk continued, "Joe, call me as a witness, and I'll instruct my clerks downstairs that if anyone appears to post the bond, they are to keep him buried in paperwork."

Not sure what my position should be, I left the courtroom to see my client in the justice center. I repeated the story for Donald, explaining to him why

I did not think that it would be wise for him to be out on the streets. I said, "You don't need to be out."

Now fear gripped me. Would Donald demand his chance for freedom? Would he create a scene in the courtroom? Harvey leaned back in his chair, his eyes locked on mine. I held my breath. Would I be sorry I ever began this whole process? Fortunately, this event was before he developed his interest in publicity. He might have found the opportunity for a feature in the *Post* attractive.

"I agree," was Harvey's only response. I told him what to expect.

Weak-kneed, I got up and left the justice center. Shortly before 2:00 P.M., I headed for the courthouse, not sure what would happen but believing the matter would be resolved successfully.

I caught my breath as I stepped into the courtroom. Television cameras, newspaper reporters, and radio reporters filled the arena. I laughed at myself for having forgotten that the prosecutor, judge, and clerk of courts were all elected officials who would go out of their way to get publicity. The judge was famous for his quote, "I don't care what they say about me, just so they spell my name correctly." I speculated as to who had called the press and later made that inquiry to each. All expressed ignorance.

The hearing began with the prosecutor calling the clerk of courts as his witness.

"Your honor," Jennings began in a deep voice, "I received an anonymous tip this morning that someone was on the way to make Donald Harvey's bond."

The prosecutor then argued that the bond should be revoked and no bond set. I, in my show for the press, argued that my client was entitled to a bond. The judge ended the hearing by ordering the bond revoked and no bond set. The press pushed past me to Jennings, intrigued by the circumstances of an anonymous phone call and Harvey's close approach to being set free.

We all returned to our respective offices, having frustrated the attempt to release the serial killer, without anyone's learning how I had participated in the affair.

Months later, I released the story. The *New York Post* categorically denied that it had ever occurred.

23. Guilty in Ohio

Ten bodies had been exhumed for forensic examination. The results had corroborated Donald Harvey's confession. Prosecutor Art Ney was convinced. He reconvened the grand jury.

The subsequent steps were a formality; the outcome was a foregone conclusion because of the plea bargain. There would be no actual trial, no arguments by the attorneys. The grand jury would decide to indict Harvey, Harvey would plead guilty to each count, and the court would announce the sentence. Nonetheless, the nine jurors and three alternates sat in stunned silence as they viewed the videotapes of Harvey's confession and of the depositions by the experts employed by the prosecutor. Although it was not their role to decide guilt or to recommend the punishment, they were overwhelmed by the revelations. They voted to indict Harvey on twenty-five counts of murder and four counts of attempted murder.

Prosecutor Art Ney had staged the formal hearing for drama. It was undoubtedly the biggest case of his career. The media responded accordingly. The press was present in force, and television crews from all over the United States and from Japan, South America, and France were in the courtroom.

The day of the plea, August 21, 1987, Judge Mathews's courtroom was packed. Families of the victims were crammed into a reserved section of the seats, and the remaining seats were filled with court and city officials and the media.

Donald had been surreptitiously moved into the court's jury room adjacent to the judge's chambers. In this room, Donald and I waited for the appointed time. Although two deputies were with us, Harvey was in hand-cuffs. Knowing what his sentence was to be because of the plea bargain, we were still apprehensive. I could think of nothing to say to reassure him. Tension mounted.

Immediately outside the door, the two short narrow halls were filled with deputies, court officials, prosecutors, press, and onlookers. I tried to maneuver through the crowd to speak to the judge about a minor detail, but I found that impossible. Normally, the back door of the judge's chambers would be closed and locked; but now, either the door had been propped open, or there were so many people moving about that the door was constantly open. Failing to get the judge's attention, I returned to the jury room. The two deputies attempted to exchange jokes, but the effort failed. While the defendant and I sat anxiously awaiting our call, the deputies stood at the ready.

Harvey asked, "What are they waiting for?"

I shrugged. I didn't know. Apparently no one knew.

Harvey's dark eyes appeared enormous, and he jumped every time the doors opened. He repeatedly asked what was happening. I didn't know, and if the deputies knew, they weren't saying.

Judge Mathews was not immune to the excitement. He appeared in the jury room with a camera and asked me to take a picture of him with the defendant. (For years, the jurist proudly displayed the photo and had it placed on his mouse pad. Later, he sent a copy to Harvey. When I told the jurist Harvey thought it looked like father and son, Judge Mathews took the picture off display and gave the mouse pad to me to turn over to Harvey.)

Rich DiAngelo, the muscular bailiff for Judge Mathews, stuck his head in the door. "It's show time."

The deputies removed Harvey's handcuffs and escorted him into the judge's chambers. The door leading to the courtroom was open and people spilled all over. Deputies and their superiors were milling about, shouting instructions. I pushed through the throng with Harvey immediately behind.

As I left the chambers for the courtroom, I felt a jerk from behind. Turning, I realized that Harvey had grabbed the back of my jacket for security. Pushing through the crowd to reach the counsel table, I found the only two empty seats left in the room. A brief smile touched my lips as we sat, realizing that our circumstances carried a few perks.

Harvey seemed frozen in place. He asked me if his sister was there. Looking around, I didn't see her; but I assured Harvey that I had seen and spoken to Pat in the courtroom before coming to the jury room. The spectators spilled out of the courtroom and down the hall, and Pat was lost to view in the crowd.

I leaned back. The room was packed with law enforcement officials and spectators. With the exception of Pat, there was not one other person in the room who was on Harvey's side. It was me against the world, and I had won. Harvey's deal was sealed. They were going through the motions now, but this was the victory dance. Although I was still not sure of some minor details, a deep sense of victory, well beyond simple satisfaction, gripped me. I might not have created the game or the rules, but I had played the hell out of the hand I was given and had come out ahead. Donald would not be executed.

Ney had choreographed the next act, and he was the star. He put on such a show that Donald whispered to me, "What is he running for?"

I whispered back, "Governor."

We both laughed briefly, an unfortunate occurrence, for we were later criticized for insensitivity.

Standing by an easel, Ney intoned each of the twenty-nine indictments. Harvey pled guilty to each.

Judge Mathews pronounced Harvey's sentence in accordance with the plea bargain: three consecutive life terms. Since the minimum time actually served for a life sentence would be twenty years, Harvey would be incarcerated for at least sixty years. He would be ninety-five years old before any possibility of release.

I had accomplished my goals for both my client and society. Harvey had escaped the death penalty. He would not be free to kill again.

The sentencing didn't end the case. Assistant Prosecutor Joe Deters told the *Cincinnati Enquirer,* "We are still checking leads. People call us with things, and we check them out. If we were to find another killing we definitely would go after him and seek the death penalty."

Harvey continued to search his memory for names and details. A routine medical test performed on him at the prison triggered his memory, because one of his forgotten victims had undergone the same procedure. He told me of two more victims at Drake hospital, a woman poisoned with cyanide and a man suffocated with a plastic bag.

I immediately informed the prosecutor's office. Responding to skeptics who said that Harvey was just coming up with more claims because he craved attention and wanted more publicity, I responded that Harvey had a vital incentive to remember. The plea bargain already reached would apply to any additional death to which he confessed. "Anything else that comes from him would just be added to his confessions, but if they find another one independently, he is a dead man." Harvey remembered four more cases.

Ney, Deters, Gaines, Lawson, and Chief Deputy Coroner Harry Bonnell went to the Southern Ohio Correctional Facility in Lucasville on January 22, 1988, and interviewed Harvey for two hours in my presence. Based on this interview, Harvey was indicted for three more counts of murder at Drake hospital: Nathaniel Watson, Doris Nally, and Henry Cody. He was indicted for three more counts of attempted murder there: Willie Johnson, Lawrence Bernsden, and Anna Hood. Johnson, who was still alive and a patient at another hospital, said that he had good memories of Harvey. "He used to take care of me, and I thought he was good."

Harvey was returned to Hamilton County Common Pleas Court, where he again faced Judge Mathews. Ney presented the six charges, and Harvey pleaded guilty to each. Judge Mathews sentenced him to twenty years to life on each of the murders and ten to twenty-five years on each of the attempted murders, the sentences to be served concurrently with the three life terms he was already serving.

Donald Harvey had now been convicted of twenty-eight counts of murder and seven counts of attempted murder in Hamilton County.

24. No Federal Charges

Although Donald had confessed to murders committed at the VA hospital, the indictments returned by the grand jury included none for deaths there. Prosecutor Art Ney had concluded that the available evidence was insufficient to support charges.

Donald's memory of those deaths had been much less specific and could not be corroborated. Donald had not confessed to causing any deaths by poisoning at the VA hospital. Dr. Spitz had said that deaths by suffocation, by reducing oxygen flow, by disconnecting equipment, or by injecting air into a vein could not be detected by forensic examination of corpses upon exhumation.

Officials at the VA hospital, while superficially cooperating with the Cincinnati police investigators, expressed a desire to have the investigation of deaths there conducted by the FBI and the U.S. attorney. VA Medical Center Director Donald Ziegenhorn said that he was awaiting a list of alleged victims from the Hamilton County Prosecutor's office before officially requesting federal intervention, but that the FBI had already started a preliminary investigation.

On September 1, 1987, the *Cincinnati Enquirer* reported that U.S. Representative Bob McEwen said he wanted a congressional hearing in Cincinnati about all events concerning Harvey's employment at the VA hospital as well as a series of earlier allegations of problems at the hospital. He was quoted as saying, "This hospital has been under attack for many years, with charges of abuse and inequality. It's time for both sides to be aired."

A critical issue in the hearing would be the circumstances of Harvey's resignation from the VA hospital. Former VA police officer John Berter told the FBI agents that he had been present when Harvey was stopped and searched and that VA police chief Daniel R. Wilson bungled the search. Harvey had been allowed to resign instead of facing a felony charge for carrying a concealed weapon because the search of his gym bag had been illegal. Berter claimed that his own firing was the result of his efforts to report shortcomings of his superior.

The official record of Harvey's leaving the VA states, "Resigned because personal reasons [sic]." There is no mention of the search that prompted his resignation.

I advised Donald not to talk with the FBI. He had nothing to gain. This was one of the two times that he didn't follow my instructions. The federal investigators interrogated Harvey for over four hours. Harvey admitted responsibility for seventeen deaths, including some that were accidental. I told them that Harvey agreed to the questioning without the protection of a plea bargain against my advice because he wanted to end the proceedings against him and begin serving his prison sentences. He had little to fear from a federal prosecution, because there was no applicable federal death penalty, and he already knew that he would be in prison for the rest of his life.

Although the federal investigation continued for a year, no charges were ever filed. I believe that the federal authorities were hesitant to move because of fears of lawsuits by the families of the victims. Harvey complained to me that the lack of action also prevented the families from receiving compensation from the Ohio state crime victim's fund, but I was powerless to change the situation. The families have never been informed.

Daniel Wilson was transferred to Lakeside Veterans Administration Hospital in Chicago as a detective, officially at his own request. He resigned after three months there. He has since been charged with making false statements in regard to his employment application and in regard to a citation that was issued with respect to Harvey.

John Berter appealed his firing, but the Office of Special Counsel rejected his appeal, ruling that he was fired for poor performance and unauthorized absences, not for blowing the whistle on Wilson. In May 1988, Berter received the ten-thousand-dollar Cavallo Prize for Courage in Business and Government, which was established by the Cavallo Foundation to recognize "people who have chosen to speak out in situations in which it would have been far easier to have remained silent." The prize was at least some compensation for his loss of his job, whether or not his whistle-blowing was a factor in his being fired.

Had Wilson followed proper procedures, the incident that resulted in Harvey's being fired would have been part of the official record. Harvey might never have applied at Drake under those circumstances. And if he had, even a cursory reference check would have prevented his being hired.

25. Guilty in Kentucky

Laurel County (Kentucky) Commonwealth Attorney Thomas Handy had reacted to my offer of a plea bargain by undertaking his own investigation. His agents determined that seventy-two deaths occurred at Marymount Hospital during Harvey's employment there. None of these deaths had been considered suspicious. Kentucky State Medical Examiner George Nichols reviewed the medical records of these seventy-two patients. Meanwhile, Handy's staff tried to locate and interview anyone who worked with Harvey there and the families of those seventy-two who had died there during that period.

Handy also attempted unsuccessfully to obtain records of the psychiatric treatment Harvey received at Cumberland River Comprehensive Care Center shortly after leaving Marymount. The circuit judge rejected his subpoena of those records, ruling that release of the records would be a violation of patient-doctor confidentiality, which is protected under Kentucky law.

Nichols' review identified ten cases that could be considered possible fits with what was known about Harvey's activities, but there was not enough evidence to classify any of those as suspicious deaths. Handy concluded that nothing would be gained by exhumation, since the likelihood of finding any useful evidence was almost nil.

Interviews with relatives and fellow workers produced no tangible evidence. Some commented unfavorably about his homosexuality, and some said that he was an unskilled beginner, but there were no suspicions of causing deaths of patients. There were no indications that the hospital administrators were negligent.

I refused to allow Kentucky officials to interview Harvey without a signed plea bargain, and Handy realized that he did not have the evidence to prosecute Harvey without a confession. He did not even know the identities of the victims.

Handy said that he had studied the Hamilton County cases and believed that Harvey would be a credible witness. He said that Kentucky would be giving up essentially nothing by agreeing to the plea bargain, because Harvey could not be executed under Kentucky law, and he was already certain to remain in jail for at least sixty years.

Handy finally replied to me with an agreement to follow Hamilton County's lead. He forwarded a plea agreement to me, and after Harvey signed, Handy signed off on Sunday, September 6, 1987, and made arrangements for a taped confession. Harvey would provide names and details of deaths he caused at Marymount Hospital and would plead guilty to any criminal charges brought by a Laurel County grand jury. Harvey also agreed to release his medical records, including the psychiatric treatment at Cumberland River. Handy would not seek the death penalty and would recommend that the sentences run concurrently with the sentences Harvey was serving in Ohio.

The Kentucky investigators came to the Hamilton County Justice Center to interview Harvey on September 9. Seven of us were crowded into a small room. Handy conducted the interrogation. Also present in addition to Harvey and me were Laurel County Sheriff Floyd Brothers and Jean Howell from his office, London Police Chief Bill Smith, and Kentucky state pathologist George Nichols.

In spite of the crowding, the situation was informal. Donald, wearing his blue prison jumpsuit, sat opposite Handy at a small table. I sat to his side, and the officers were seated behind Donald, outside his line of vision. The men wore short-sleeved shirts, and Ms. Howell wore a bright yellow dress.

Handy, a handsome man with a well-trimmed mustache, was gracious and almost kindly in his manner. His soft southern accent contrasted pleasantly with his subject. Harvey was poised and coherent and expressed his willingness to cooperate. After conferring briefly with me, Donald gave all his attention to Handy. I was comfortable with the arrangements and even felt free to leave the room briefly during the interrogation to take care of other business.

Handy began by questioning Harvey about his personal history. Harvey answered freely, but was hazy on a few details. He apologized, saying that he had four shock treatments when he was a patient at the VA hospital in Lexington and it affected his memory of some events around that time.

About three-quarters of an hour into the interview, Handy started asking Harvey about his duties at Marymount Hospital, focusing first on his handling of oxygen tanks. Harvey explained about storage, connecting the tanks in the patients' rooms, and reading the pressure gauges.

When they shifted to discussing the deaths of patients, Harvey said that he had killed one with a coat hanger inserted through his catheter, two by smothering them with pillows, and nine or ten by cutting off their oxygen supply, primarily by using bad valves. He remembered in detail the room numbers, medical conditions, and general descriptions of the patients, but he was unable to recall their names. He repeatedly referred to a patient by the name of Philpott and tried to identify which one he was. Handy had a list of fourteen names, and he and Harvey tried to match the information Harvey had with the names on the list. Harvey finally decided that Philpott might be McFadden.

Repeatedly during the discussion, Harvey referred to his youth, inexperience, and lack of training. He pointed out that he did not know how to deal with patients who were irrational or having psychiatric problems. Handy suggested that all of the deaths Harvey caused at Marymount were spur-of-the-moment, not planned, and Harvey agreed. Harvey said that some of the deaths were accidental, not intentional, but he acknowledged responsibility. He said he was remorseful and felt sorry for the families of the people he killed. He offered to apologize to them.

Handy terminated the interview after six hours and forty-four minutes.

They met again on October 21. In the interim, Handy had matched medical records with the information Harvey had provided in the previous interview and had developed a tentative list of Harvey's victims. A casual observer might well have thought that Handy and Harvey were colleagues conferring on a mutual project except that Handy was dressed in a suit and Harvey was wearing his jail uniform. They sat at the corner of a table, pouring over a pile of documents. Handy presented his conclusions to Harvey, and they checked the information against Harvey's memory. Several names that Harvey remembered turned out to be names of relatives of the victims. William Bowling's daughter was named McFadden.

They agreed upon a list of thirteen victims.

Handy determined that eleven of the deaths could be classified as first-degree murder. He said the other two might not be properly called accidental, but that they did not involve criminal liability on Harvey's part. Kentucky Medical Examiner Dr. Nichols confirmed the earlier opinion that exhumation would yield no useful information.

Although Harvey had already been examined by psychiatrists in connection with the cases in Hamilton County and ruled sane to stand trial, Handy made the conservative decision to have a new examination for Kentucky. He chose to engage Dr. Tanay because his prior experience with Harvey would facilitate the process.

Dr. Tanay interviewed Harvey again the next day. He referred to the previous interview and indicated that he was pleased to have the opportunity to talk with Harvey again without the constraints of the first interview, when the immunity granted to Harvey by his plea bargain did not apply to the deaths in Kentucky. Harvey was relaxed and smiling.

Dr. Tanay asked Harvey why he had decided to confess to the deaths in Laurel County. Donald replied that he wanted to get it over with and get on with his life—a strange remark since "getting on with his life" meant sixty years in prison in Ohio. In response to probing by Dr. Tanay, he said that he was following his attorney's advice. He assured Dr. Tanay that he was well satisfied with his attorney and considered me a friend. He said that the only time he had gone against my advice was talking to the FBI about the deaths at the VA hospital. He confirmed that he understood the plea bargain for Laurel County.

In this interview, Dr. Tanay reviewed Harvey's childhood history and asked about his getting the job at Marymount and his training there. He explored Harvey's homosexuality in some depth, concentrating on the time he was at Marymount.

Focusing on Harvey's relationship with Vernon Midden, Dr. Tanay apparently placed much significance on the fact that Midden was a funeral director. He repeatedly returned to probing the idea that sex and death were connected for Harvey. Harvey denied that having sexual encounters with Midden at the funeral home had any special meaning. He said they engaged in sexual activity three or four times a week, and the funeral home was just a convenient place. He said that Midden had oral sex with other young men when they were lying in a casket, but that he refused to participate in that way. In response to specific questions, Harvey told Dr. Tanay that he never had any fantasies of death and sex together. Occult practices did not come up in this interview.

Dr. Tanay also looked for any periodicity among the deaths caused by Harvey, but he found no patterns.

At the conclusion of the interview, Donald told Dr. Tanay that he was looking forward to being settled in prison, getting a job there, and perhaps going to school. It seemed to me that statement could be interpreted as either an unwillingness to face reality or a remarkable acceptance of the inevitable. I don't know what Dr. Tanay concluded from it, but Donald's adjustment to prison life suggests the latter view.

Donald Harvey recently told a story about this interview that had not been previously revealed. He had looked up information about Dr. Tanay in preparation for meeting with him again. During the course of the interview, he brought up details of Dr. Tanay's personal history in order to make a point about his disagreement with some of the things Dr. Tanay was concluding about him. Dr. Tanay was obviously offended. Donald said that after the conclusion of the interview and off the record, Tanay said, "You son of a bitch."

Dr. Tanay reported to Handy that Harvey was competent to stand trial, that he was knowledgeable about the legal process, and that he had been legally sane during his employment at Marymount Hospital.

Handy convened a grand jury in Laurel County and presented to them videotapes of his interview with Harvey. Although Harvey had confessed to killing thirteen patients, only ten victims could be corroborated. Three of his claimed victims could not be identified. Handy concluded one of the ten was not a homicide.

The grand jury returned indictments on eight counts of murder: William Bowling, Maude Nichols, Viola Wyan, Silas Butner, John Combs, Maggie Rawlins, Ben Gilbert, and Elizabeth Wyatt. They returned one indictment of voluntary manslaughter: Eugene McQueen. Donald Harvey pleaded guilty to all nine counts. Circuit Court Judge Lewis Hopper sentenced him to life in prison for each murder and twenty years for manslaughter, the sentences to be served in Ohio concurrently with the three life terms for convictions in Hamilton County.

26. Civil Suits

As soon as the Hamilton County grand jury had returned its indictments and Donald Harvey had pled guilty, attorneys for the families of the victims rushed to file civil suits against him, the hospitals, hospital administrators and trustees, and various medical staffs. Eighteen suits, some of them class actions, were filed in Hamilton County, asking for a total of more than $235 million.

Donald was unconcerned about the suits. I told him that suing him was an exercise in futility, because he had no assets. In legal terms, he was "judgment proof." Including him as a defendant was, however, a legal requirement. For his part, he was quite willing to provide depositions to assist in the suits, declaring that he wanted the families of the victims to be compensated. In this stance, he was inconsistent with some earlier comments, when he had been critical of some of the families for lack of attention to the patients. I cautioned him to reveal nothing that he had not already given to the investigators in the criminal cases.

The attorneys apparently anticipated a bonanza, expecting that Harvey would write a book about his killings. According to Ohio law, any payments to Harvey for a book would be seized to satisfy claims against him. Donald, however, never had any intention of writing a book, although he wanted a book to be written.

Donald asked me to be his attorney for the civil cases. As his court-appointed public defender, I was paid by Hamilton County and the state of Ohio for defending him in the criminal suit, but there were no provisions for me to be paid for defense in the civil suits. Neither Donald nor his family had funds to pay me, nor did they have any incentive; because in view of his confessions in the criminal cases, he had no defense. I, however, would not abandon Donald. I wanted to be sure that nothing developed in the testimony for the civil suits would place him at risk for an additional criminal trial in which he was not protected by the plea bargain. I was especially concerned about deaths at the VA hospital, since Hamilton County had taken no action on those.

My sticking with Donald for the civil suits was not entirely altruistic. I had developed a unique relationship with him and was anticipating writing this book. I did not want another attorney to be involved with his cases. I told Harvey that I would represent him, even though without compensation, and filed the necessary papers in the clerk's office designating myself as trial counsel.

Although Donald was not concerned about the civil suits, I knew that there was a potential trap. The plea bargain protected Harvey for only the deaths to which he had confessed. If the civil cases should uncover that Harvey was responsible for any other deaths, he was in jeopardy for criminal prosecution that could result in a death sentence. Harvey's memory was not perfect. He had remembered three murders and three attempted murders after his initial confession, and they had been added to his confession covered by the plea bargain. If the prosecutors should find another murder independently, he was unprotected.

The vague threat became tangible on March 1, 1988, when the attorney for Shelton Gillispie, widower of Ruth Gillispie and executor of her estate, filed suit for $25 million compensatory damages and $50 million punitive damages against Donald Harvey, Daniel Drake Memorial Hospital, Jan Taylor, and the board of Hamilton County Commissioners.

Harvey had not confessed to causing Ruth Gillispie's death, and her case was not covered by the plea bargain. Although Gillispie had been a patient at Drake Hospital and had died there, and Harvey had provided some of her care, he repeatedly denied that he had injured her in any way. I recalled that in his confession he had mentioned her by name and stated explicitly that he did nothing to harm her. He said that she was a difficult patient who accused nurses and assistants of trying to poison her when they gave her medicines, but that he never gave her any poison and she had not singled him out as one whom she accused.

Ironically, he had assisted in her autopsy.

Although the prosecutor's staff investigated the claims, they found no evidence to connect Harvey to any criminal act in connection with Gillispie's death. The plaintiff asked for an order to exhume the body for forensic examination, but the court resisted that motion, urging the parties to reach a settlement out of court. In October 1991, an agreement was reached. The amount of the settlement is confidential, but was reported to be $45,000. Harvey, of course, was responsible for none of the payment. For Harvey, the important item was the inclusion of a clause releasing him from any liability. No criminal charges were filed.

The other civil cases in Hamilton County were pooled for a negotiated settlement. At the first meeting of the attorneys with the judge, twelve attorneys were present. The judge remarked, "My God, with this many attorneys we won't even get an agreement as to what day it is." In fact, there was little acrimony. On Harvey's behalf, I confessed judgment, which meant that he would offer no defense. This concession saved much time and expense without harm to Harvey, because he had already given a full confession in the criminal cases.

The eventual settlement between the plaintiffs and Hamilton County was for $2.3 million. The judgment against Donald Harvey personally was for $11 million. I tried to make it less, but the attorneys for the plaintiffs had not given up on the idea that Harvey might write a book that would have multimillion dollars in sales. With Harvey's lack of assets, the dollar figure of the judgment is meaningless.

Civil cases in Kentucky followed a far different pattern. Seventeen years had elapsed, and evidence was much harder to obtain. Harvey was at essentially no risk that any cases not covered by his plea bargain might arise. The deaths investigated in the criminal cases depended upon his confession.

The first civil suit against Harvey in Kentucky was filed more than four months after Harvey's guilty plea and sentencing. Defendants in that suit and in seven more subsequently filed were Donald Harvey and Nazareth Literary and Benevolent Institution, which ran Marymount Hospital.

Although I was admitted to the bar in Kentucky as well as Ohio, I chose not to be present in the court in Kentucky. Since Donald was not at risk, I had no incentive to devote the time or to incur the expense for the court appearances. Harvey would also not be present, because he could not leave Ohio. The court appointed a guardian ad litem (a representative for someone who cannot speak for himself) for Harvey, but Harvey refused to have anything to do with him, and he eventually resigned with court permission.

The legal process in Kentucky was long and tedious. The attorneys generated mountains of paperwork. Donald received copies of everything and delighted in receiving all that mail in prison. He passed the documents along to me, and we met several times to discuss what action he should take. He accepted my suggestion that he not respond to anything. As I anticipated, this strategy eventually resulted in a default judgment against him, which had the same effect as formally confessing judgment in court—but required no effort.

Nazareth Literary and Benevolent Institution chose as an initial defense strategy to challenge the suits on the basis that the statute of limitations had run out and asked for a summary judgment against the plaintiffs. The circuit court agreed and issued the summary judgment. The plaintiffs immediately appealed. The appeals court reversed the ruling of the circuit court and returned the case to it.

The plaintiffs then asked to take depositions from Harvey. After more legal wrangling, that request was approved. Initially, Harvey tried to refuse to say anything as long as his name was listed as a defendant, but he was told that change was not feasible. He relented because of his position that he wanted the victims' families to be compensated.

Since Harvey was in prison in Ohio, the authorities there would allow the deposition to be taken only if the Kentucky attorneys would come to the prison for the purpose. Accordingly, the attorneys chose a representative group to make the trip to Lebanon, Ohio, to take the deposition. Harvey cooperated and gave full disclosure.

A delegation from Kentucky came to Ohio and took a deposition from him at the Warren County Correctional Institution. I attended when this deposition was taken, although I felt that Harvey really had had no need for me in these cases. There were no deaths not already covered by the plea bargain.

Marcia Rydings, attorney for Nazareth, repeatedly asked Harvey whether he told anyone at the hospital about his actions in killing patients. His responses were invariably negative.

Ultimately, the suits against the hospital were dismissed. A default judgment was taken against Harvey. The Kentucky legislature passed special legislation to waive the statute of limitations with regard to the state's victims' assistance program, making each family eligible for a maximum of $25,000 compensation.

None of the civil suits ever went to trial.

PART IV

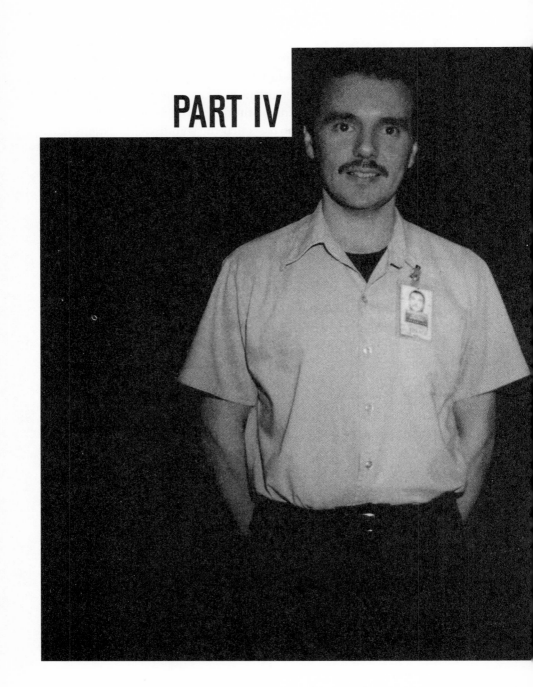

THE REST
OF THE STORY

27. Fallout

Donald Harvey had additional victims to whom he had caused no physical harm. These were the people who suffered because his actions disclosed failures in their job performance that would have been considered minor, if discovered, except for the spotlight shone on them by publicity surrounding Harvey. There also were people who acted defensively and improperly to reduce the glare of that spotlight.

The *Cincinnati Post*, in an editorial on August 19, 1987, titled "Why wasn't he stopped?" expressed the public view: "How could it have happened when Harvey's employment background contained bright red warning flags? If hiring and firing practices at two local hospitals had been more rigorous, the killer might not have found it so easy to continue a career looking after helpless patients."

After commenting that the VA hospital permitted Harvey to resign instead of firing him and that Drake officials made only a cursory check on his past performance, the *Post* continued: "The administrators of Veterans and Drake hospitals probably did not behave very differently from most employers in taking the easy way out. What company or institution hasn't made a similar deal to get rid of a problem worker? In these litigious times, employers necessarily worry about being sued by disgruntled former employees. Nor is Drake unusual in failing to seek thorough accounts of a lowly applicant's history in previous jobs. . . . Still, Donald Harvey's crimes must prompt a rethinking of policies at Veterans and Drake and hospitals everywhere. There is no escaping the knowledge that in this case, lax personnel practices had unspeakable consequences for a great many people."

A committee of the Cincinnati Board of Health considered a proposal to require police checks on new nursing home personnel. The proposed action was rejected as impractical and too costly.

During a meeting on August 2, 1987, the county commissioners and Drake trustees discussed firing or reassigning some of the Drake administrators and appointed a three-person committee to make a recommendation.

Elaine Mann, a switchboard operator at Drake, led a petition campaign gathering support from other Drake employees, patients, and visitors for the chief executive officer, Jan Taylor. Other employees called the effort coercive and unethical. Hamilton County Commissioner Norman Murdock, who was also a Drake trustee, was angered by the circulation of the petition. He considered it inappropriate and cited permitting it as further evidence of Taylor's incompetence.

In a tense three-hour meeting on September 10, the trustees voted four to two to retain Taylor, with a proviso that his performance would be closely monitored. Two supervisors left the hospital for unspecified reasons: acting medical director Dr. Walter Matern resigned, and Daisy Key, Harvey's nursing supervisor, who was on sick leave and scheduled to retire, did not return to work. Ann Moreton, assistant personnel director, was demoted because she had failed to check on Harvey's record at the VA hospital.

The Joint Commission on Accreditation of Healthcare Organizations advanced the date of its next scheduled inspection by eight months, conducting a surprise inspection on September 23. Following a seven-hour visit, the inspectors made a few recommendations for improvements and announced that accreditation would be continued.

Relief at passing this inspection was short-lived. The U.S. Department of Health and Human Services requested a special inspection. An eight-member team from the Ohio Department of Health's Bureau of Medical Services arrived for a nine-day examination of personnel policies, hospital supervisory rules, pharmacy procedures, food services, staffing, and record keeping. The inspectors cited deficiencies in governing, security for medicine carts, therapeutic diets, activities, resident rights, rehabilitative services, social services, medical records, and patient care management. They recommended decertification for Medicare and Medicaid funding.

On December 3, the hospital was informed that it would lose certification to treat Medicare patients and some Medicaid patients, effective January 9.

The hospital appealed, claiming that many of the deficiencies had been addressed, and a re-inspection was scheduled to take place late in December.

A Hamilton County grand jury indicted Jan Taylor on December 30 for four counts of tampering with evidence in Donald Harvey's personnel file during the investigation of deaths at Drake hospital. He was released from custody on his own recognizance. The Drake trustees immediately suspended him with pay and appointed a three-member team to run the hospital while the trustees searched for an interim manager. The trustees selected Barry Singleton, administrator of corporate services at the University of Cincinnati College of Medicine, for the position.

Federal officials granted Drake a thirty-day extension of certification, until February 8.

The Drake trustees voted to fire Taylor and to authorize Singleton to make extensive changes in the administration, including replacing five managers and hiring up to ten new managers. The hospital started developing a plan to transfer twenty-five to thirty patients to other facilities when certification expired on February 8.

At his trial on April 13, 1988, Jan Taylor pleaded no contest to falsification of a public document as part of a plea bargain substituting that charge for the four counts of tampering with evidence. According to Taylor's defense attorney, Taylor had added handwritten notes to Harvey's file, indicating that two of his former employers had told Drake representatives that he was eligible for rehire. This information was apparently true, but Taylor had not dated the entries, which were made on April 3 (the day before Harvey was arrested). The file thus implied incorrectly that the reference checks had been made at the time of hiring.

Taylor was sentenced to 180 days in jail, with 150 days suspended, and a year of probation. Taylor, through his attorney, requested an alternative sentence of thirty days counseling drug-dependent adolescents at a private residential rehabilitation center. His request was denied.

Taylor was incarcerated at the Hamilton County Justice Center. He took advantage of a program of double credit for working at a designated chore and reduced his service to fifteen days by washing patrol cars. He later went from a $100,000 a year job as hospital administrator to a $20,000 a year job as a construction supervisor.

Drake hospital passed re-inspection in July 1988 and regained certification.

28. Made for Television

The melding of Donald Harvey's story with television was a natural. The mix started with Pat Minarcin's seminal report on Cincinnati's Channel 9 before anyone else realized there was a story. As the revelations of Harvey's murders fascinated the public, the media coverage filled the television screens and the front pages of newspapers.

On September 1, 1987, two weeks after Donald's appearance for the grand jury and his conviction and sentencing, the *Ira Joe Fisher Show* on Channel 12 was devoted entirely to the case. Ira Joe's normally jovial round face took on a serious mien as he introduced the subject.

Guests were Art Ney, Dr. Walter Lippert, Channel 12 troubleshooter Howard Ain, and me. We were seated in the traditional semicircle favored by talk shows.

Ira Joe took me first. A suspicious person might have thought we were color-coordinated by a producer. Ira Joe wore a camel-colored jacket and dark tie, and I wore a light blue jacket and gray tie. His shirt was the light blue then customary for television appearances, although that technical requirement went out with the advent of color television.

He asked me how I became Donald's defense attorney, how I learned that he was responsible for multiple deaths instead of just the one he was charged with, and why I initiated a plea bargain. I gave him straightforward answers without editorializing. He didn't flinch when I made several references to Channel 9. I wasn't deliberately trying to promote Pat Minarcin, but his special report was an essential part of my account.

Ira Joe then asked Art Ney why he accepted the offer of a plea bargain.

Art made quite a speech about the absence of any *corpus delicti* for any case except that of John Powell. He explained that the police had at that time no material evidence of any other crime—no corpse of a murder victim and no physical evidence to support a confession of murder. He stressed that this case was the reverse of ninety-nine percent of murder cases.

He summarized much of the testimony by Drs. Blanke and Spitz. He dwelt dramatically on how an air embolism could be detected by performing an autopsy underwater. I thought that unnecessary, since that kind of death was not an issue in this case. However, his presentation was good theater, and he was referring to a time before Donald's confession, when the prosecutors didn't know his means of killing. He emphasized that false confessions are common.

Ney said that they needed to know who the victims were, and only Harvey knew that. He said there were 172 possible victims, and it was not feasible to disinter all of them to confirm the deaths Harvey might have caused. He would have been looking for the eleven who had been poisoned with arsenic. Poisonings with cyanide, rat poison, and adhesive cleaner could not be detected by autopsies on embalmed bodies, nor could deaths by suffocation or shutting off oxygen flow.

He concluded by declaring he was convinced that accepting the plea bargain was the right move.

Dr. Lippert was next. He presented a lecture on the psychology of serial killers. As he talked in generalizations, he did not make it clear that he had interviewed Harvey himself. He stressed that such persons superficially appear normal, but are not.

Ira Joe interrupted to ask me why we didn't offer a plea of insanity. I answered that I had considered such a plea, but Harvey did not meet the criteria, according to state law. Dr. Lippert agreed with me. He continued with his generalizations about serial killers.

Howard Ain commented on Dr. Lehman's chance discovery that John Powell had been poisoned with cyanide. Art Ney said how fortunate his discovery had been and indicated that without it Harvey might still be killing patients at Drake. Ain suggested that Harvey might have been trying to get caught, pointing out that Harvey had to have known that there would be an autopsy.

Ira Joe asked me for my opinion on that idea, and I responded that I believed what Donald had told me—that he did not expect the pathologist to look for anything but confirmation of the brain injury that had put Powell in the hospital. Dr. Lippert pointed out that serial killers enjoy theater. Although Lippert was generalizing, I thought that certainly fit Donald.

Ira Joe had another guest, Michael Pike, the son of Joe Pike, who was one of Harvey's victims. Michael had organized a group of families of victims to work for public awareness of the possibility of murders of their loved ones in terminal-care facilities. Michael said that his family had reconciled themselves to his father's death from pneumonia, but the revelation that he had been murdered generated emotional turmoil.

A phone line was activated for callers. The first caller asked if the families of all victims had been notified. Ney answered that immediately after the indictments, he had called all the families of victims into his office to inform them of what had happened. He had arranged for grief counselors to be present. He said he could not include survivors of victims for whom Harvey was not indicted. That means that the identities of Harvey's victims at the VA hospital have never been made public.

Jan Taylor, administrator of Drake hospital, had been invited to be on the program but had declined because of the ongoing police investigation. Ira Joe reported that Taylor had said that an intensive internal investigation was in progress.

A caller asked if there were reasons to be concerned about other persons working in hospital settings. Dr. Lippert replied that it was very difficult to screen applicants for homicidal tendencies. He said that people with such tendencies would fool the ordinary employment supervisors; only an expert such as himself could pick up on the subtle clues that would disclose the risk.

Throughout the program, occasional clips from Harvey's sentencing were shown on the screen. The pictures usually showed Donald and me conferring. Donald looked calm and in control. In fact, he looked less agitated than I did. The *Sacramento Bee* picked up one of those pictures and ran it on the front page. A casual observer would have thought Donald was the attorney and I was the defendant.

Donald Harvey's story reached a national television audience when San Francisco TV station KTVU produced the documentary, *Angel of Death*. Fox network distributed the program, sponsored by AT&T. The show aired on October 11, 1987.

Bob MacKenzie narrated the presentation. His casual, windblown appearance served to increase the impact of the pictures shown on the screen. The show began with a few overly dramatic hospital shots. Throughout the show, the scene returned to show Harvey, in shackles, being escorted down the corridor of the courthouse by deputies.

The documentary contained a number of errors. I suppose that was inevitable, considering the relatively short production time and the fact that it preceded the court action in Kentucky. Also, faced with such a tremendous amount of information, the television producers necessarily made choices of what to include. I would have made more balanced choices.

MacKenzie implied that John Powell, after a long period of treatments in the hospital, was recovering from his head injury when Harvey killed him. Such was not the case. Powell had taken a serious turn for the worse and his death was expected.

The program also minimized the events leading to Harvey's arrest, a critical part of the whole story.

The importance of Pat Minarcin's Channel 9 special was given a full treatment. MacKenzie interviewed Pat and showed major excerpts from that show. Pat's individual role and his journalistic courage didn't get the emphasis I thought he deserved. Of course, MacKenzie had no way to know of our clandestine meetings leading up to Pat's special.

Prosecutor Art Ney declined to participate. Assistant Prosecutor Joe Deters was interviewed throughout the program and came across very well. The survivors of the victims were vocal in their criticisms of the plea bargain.

Pictures of exhumations wisely showed the overall activity and left the details to the imagination of the viewers. I think Art Ney and Joe Deters must have been pleased with the demonstration that each exhumation was a major operation, not to be undertaken lightly.

Just before the commercial break, the camera showed a picture of Pat Minarcin interviewing Donald in the jail. This episode was a dramatic demonstration of security measures, because they were required to face each other through a bulletproof window and talk by phone. Their conversation stressed the mercy-killing angle.

After the break, the scene shifted to rural Kentucky. The three-room house in which Donald grew up and the similar house in which Donald's mother,

Goldie, now lives were shown in their isolation. He showed a series of pictures of Donald as a healthy, happy child, showing plainly his apparent normalcy.

MacKenzie interviewed Goldie against the background of her present home. She expressed sympathy for the survivors of Donald's victims and said, "I also lost a son."

Goldie said she was unaware until very recently of the sexual abuse Donald suffered as a child. She said that had she known, she would have put a stop to it. She said both Donald's father and his sister, Pat, did know. Pat confirmed her awareness, adding that back then she thought her knowing Donald's secret formed a bond between them.

MacKenzie interviewed Donald's high school principal, Martha Turner. She said that Donald was a good student and showed no signs of any problems at school or, to her knowledge, at home. She said the school had counseling services available but had perceived no need for them for Donald. MacKenzie missed the circumstances of Donald's leaving school, thinking Donald had left voluntarily to accelerate his graduation.

When MacKenzie switched to talking about Marymount, he made another error. He said that the first death Harvey caused at Marymount was an accident. That made a better story, but in fact the first death, although Harvey was not indicted for it, was intentional. The second death was an accident.

MacKenzie interviewed Laurel County Prosecutor Tom Handy but, since this was before the convictions in Kentucky, the interview was not very productive.

Dr. Tanay, in an interview with MacKenzie, either forgot what he knew about Donald Harvey or was so intent upon advancing his own theories that he ignored the facts. He said that, like the typical serial killer, Harvey chose victims of a type. He said that in Harvey's case, the type was "helpless male." Since thirteen of Harvey's victims were female, this categorization was obviously wrong. Tanay also said that the reason Harvey killed no one at the Veterans Administration hospital while he was working in the morgue was that his need for association with death was met by his job. Harvey's explanation that he had no access to live patients when he was a morgue assistant makes more sense, especially since he did kill outside the hospital during that time.

A major segment of the show was MacKenzie interviewing Harvey in jail. The setting was again the use of phones between participants separated by bulletproof glass. Donald was poised and pleasant. He frequently reflected before answering questions, but did not seem reluctant or evasive. Following my instructions, he refused to answer some questions.

Surprisingly, he denied to MacKenzie that childhood sexual abuse was responsible for the way he turned out as an adult.

Donald said that he likes order and discipline, and he spoke favorably of life in jail.

In response to direct questions, Donald said that he believes in God and Satan. He refused further comments on Satanism. He said that he does believe in the occult but denied that his occult beliefs influenced his killing. Inconsistency has never seemed a problem for Donald. Of course, MacKenzie knew nothing of Donald's belief in his otherworld guide, Duncan, so he had no basis for challenging that statement. Donald never referred to Duncan in any confession or deposition. Did Donald really believe that Duncan chose victims for him? I don't know, so I'm not sure to whom Donald lied about this subject.

Donald refused, as I had instructed him, to say anything about deaths in Kentucky, because those cases were not settled at the time of the interview.

He defended deaths at Drake as being mercy killings. He admitted that deaths he caused outside the hospitals were not. He said that two were to protect Carl. He went into some detail about killing Henry Hoeweler, reporting how Hoeweler had asked to die.

Donald said that he regrets some of the deaths he caused. He said that he wouldn't kill out of anger again, but that for many of the mercy killings, if given the opportunity he would do the same thing again.

He said he was now at peace with himself. Asked for a final statement, he replied that he wanted the families of the people he killed to know that he was a caring person. He cared for the people he killed and he cared for their families.

Channel 9 continued to follow Donald Harvey after he was in the penitentiary. Anchorman Clyde Gray interviewed him at the Warren County Correctional Institution in Lebanon, Ohio. Gray asked him, "How many people have you killed?"

Harvey replied without hesitation, "Eighty-seven."

I don't know where that number came from. He was convicted of thirty-six murders and one intentional manslaughter. I suspect he just added an arbitrary fifty. Certainly there were more murders than those for which he was convicted, but even he doesn't know how many.

Gray didn't pursue the number except to ask him if he knew who they were.

"I know their names."

Gray mentioned the teaching video Harvey made in 1989 to help train hospital personnel to prevent killings by staff members and showed excerpts from the tape.

Gray challenged his assertion of mercy killings, Harvey attempted to justify himself. He said that as a child he was held down and raped, and he couldn't stand to see anyone tied down. When terminally ill patients were tied in their beds, he put them out of their misery.

That statement was a contradiction of what he had told MacKenzie, when he said that sexual abuse as a child was not a factor in his killings. As on other occasions, Donald seemed unconcerned about being inconsistent.

Harvey said, "I was Dr. Kevorkian without a license."

Although Gray had said that the methods Harvey used to kill helpless patients didn't sound merciful to him, he didn't point out that Dr. Kevorkian's clients had a choice; Harvey made the choice for them.

Harvey said, "I never considered myself a killer."

"What would you call yourself?"

The answer came after a pause. "Donald Harvey."

Perhaps that was the best answer anyone could give. Donald defies classification.

News reporter Joe Webb interviewed Harvey for Channel 9 at the Warren County Correctional Institution in 1991, four years after his convictions in Ohio.

Harvey told him that when he first killed a patient at Marymount Hospital in Kentucky, he realized that he had just killed Donald Harvey. (See chapter 7.)

Webb was particularly interested in talking about Raphael Giron, a patient at Drake who had been indicted for murder but had been found incompetent to stand trial. Joe had somehow found out that Giron was on Harvey's list of potential victims. He was intrigued that I was also Giron's defense attorney.

That led to Webb's asking, "Would you kill someone like Giron today if you could?"

"No, I think they should serve their time. Killing them would be giving them the easy way out."

Donald was again being inconsistent with his own actions. He had eagerly accepted a lifetime in prison in preference to a risk of a death sentence and had adjusted well to the prison environment.

In response to a question about killing terminally ill patients, Harvey replied, "I still believe that I was right."

Harvey continues to be of interest to the media. On February 5, 2003, Scott Pelley interviewed him as part of a *60 Minutes II* feature on health-care workers who killed patients. After asking the usual questions about how many he had killed and the methods he used, Pelley asked, "How did you get away with that for seventeen years?"

"The doctors were overworked. Sometimes they didn't even see the patients after they died. They just signed the death certificates."

Pelley told the audience that others had killed to decrease their own workload. He used the expression, "Killers like Harvey," which I thought inappropriate. He, like so many others, seemed to think they could reduce Donald to a generalization.

Pelley asked Donald how he felt after killing a patient. Donald said he was glad that he didn't get caught and felt relief. He said he liked being in control.

"What about power. Did you feel powerful?"

"Power and control are the same thing. If you are in control, you have power."

Pelley asked, "Do you have regrets?"

"I regret getting caught."

After hours of videotaped confessions and depositions, Donald had become accustomed to the eye of the camera. He had developed a polished technique for positioning himself and talking to an unseen audience. An actor who projected warmth and sincerity had supplanted the haunted, wild-eyed trapped prisoner of his first television appearance.

I viewed this transformation with some trepidation. Donald enjoyed his role. He had become a celebrity. Infamous instead of famous, but a celebrity. With his new confidence, he had become more independent of me. I felt that he lacked the judgment to use that independence wisely and feared that he would exceed safe limits in dealing with the media. He asked for a copy of the *Guinness World Records,* and he was disappointed at not finding his name in the book.

Donald displayed his interest in media attention in his letters to me from prison. Here are some excerpts.

JANUARY 4, 1990 – ". . . did the *Cincinnati Post* do an end-of-the-decade for the 1980s? I saw the articles the *Cincinnati Enquirer* did. The picture of little old me was terrible."

MARCH 17, 1991 – "My interview was not on *Current Affairs* last Thursday. I still don't know why. Do you?"

MARCH 31, 1991 – "Ms. Julia Bush, our unit manager, was here to see me on 3/2/91 about an interview with Steve Dunlap or Dupont (I can't remember his last name). He was from Fox network. I told them to call you about that, it was okay from me, but they need your permission. Ms. Bush said he had been trying to set up an interview for a while."

MARCH 25, 1991 – "Did you see my interview on *Current Affairs* last Wed., 3/21/91? Did you ever hear if my interview was in the *Columbus Dispatch?* I have heard or seen nothing."

APRIL 19, 1992 – "I finally received *Medical Murders.* [There's a] picture of me. . . . I was in *True Detective* and *Front Page Detective.* I saw *Front Page Detective* but not *True Detective.*"

MAY 17, 1992 – "Here's an envelope and letter from Richard T. Griffiths of CNN. I give my permission for an interview if it's alright by you. Please let him know whatever you decide."

JULY 5, 1992 – "I have heard nothing from CNN, either. They are slow or haven't made up their mind if they want to interview or not."

AUGUST 2, 1992 – Sandy Crawford brought over some papers for me to sign for the two interviews, NBC 8/18/92 and CNN 8/28/92. She told me you were aware and had approved the interviews. I signed the papers. . . . The August issue of *Cincinnati Magazine* mentioned you in their 1987 section of their twenty-fifth anniversary issue section. It was a story about the Harvey murders."

SEPTEMBER 15, 1992 – "If *20/20 News* show wants an interview, it is okay by me. As long as you agree."

SEPTEMBER 27, 1992 – "*NBC News* was here Tuesday morning to tape me walking across the yard up to the visiting room. Just the cameraman came. It took maybe ten minutes at most. I had a two-day-old beard.

Otherwise I looked okay. When I gave the interview, you remember I was rushed out due to court time. I gave him a nice wiggle."

SEPTEMBER 29, 1992 – "I will give an interview to Professor Ronald Holmes if it is okay with you. I don't see any problem with it. . . . It is okay by me for WAKY-TV Channel 32 reporter Bruce Dumbar to visit with Professor Holmes."

DECEMBER 6, 1992 – "Have you heard if the CNN interview will be on this month? Any news about the NBC one for January?"

DECEMBER 20, 1992 – "I thought the CNN interview was scheduled for December! Have you heard when or if the CNN interview or the NBC interview will be shown?"

JANUARY 4, 1993 – "Did you see the interview I gave CNN last night? If not, it was on at 9:00 P.M., listed as "Murder by Number." The show was one hour. I didn't see it, but I heard about it from *USA News Today* and *TV Guide,* and the C.O.s were talking about it."

JANUARY 21, 1993 – I didn't see the CNN interview. I heard the second part was about me more. From what I'm told, I didn't make an ass of myself."

FEBRUARY 7, 1993 – Did Channel 5 ever contact you? I haven't heard anything since I wrote you last week."

APRIL 5, 1993 – "I sent a letter to you concerning the *America's Most Wanted.* Did you get it? Whatever you decided to do is cool with me."

APRIL 18, 1993 – "I talked with my mother Saturday. The people from *America's Most Wanted* had talked with her at Lexington, Ky., last week. They also had talked with Pat on camera or off. I don't know yet. I think she let them borrow a couple of pictures. . . . Since I haven't heard anything so far, I guess the interview is still on for the 24th of April."

JULY 18, 1993 – "Mom said I was in the *National Examiner,* one of the gossip rags. Plus a C.O. said he saw it. Who wrote it, I don't know! Do you know anything about it? I don't recall every magazine of that nature. Have you ever read the *National Examiner?*"

FEBRUARY 12, 2003 – "Did you see the three minutes or less I was on *60 Minutes* last Wednesday? That was a joke . . . why spend thousands of dollars for three minutes?"

MAY 27, 2003 – "My mom said she had been told by some of her neighbors that there had been filmmakers from New York filming and asking questions about me. . . No one really knows why they were filming. One said they were doing a movie. Have you been contacted about anything of this nature?"

Donald Harvey achieved the notoriety he desired. The media accorded him the status of being considered the prototypical hospital serial killer, the one to whom all others are compared. Sixteen years after Harvey's conviction, a breaking news story directed attention to Harvey again. Charles Cullen, a nurse who was suspected of killing one patient, admitted to multiple killings at hospitals in New Jersey and western Pennsylvania. The New Jersey *Star-Ledger* sent reporter Mike Frassinelli to Lebanon to interview Harvey in the penitentiary. I sat in on the interview.

Donald considers the interview with Frassinelli a waste of time. He doubted that Frassinelli really came for a story. Donald said, "After seventeen years, I didn't have anything to tell him." Donald had not read or heard anything about Cullen before the interview. Neither Donald nor I ever saw anything in print as a result of the interview. Frassinelli questioned Donald at some length about one particular death, mentioning in passing that he knew the son of the victim. Donald thinks that inquiry was really the purpose of the visit.

John Kasich interviewed me about Cullen on the Fox News national television program, *Heartland.*

The stories of Charles Cullen and Donald Harvey are eerily similar. Each of them had caused the deaths of hospital patients for many years without the deaths having been classified homicides, although both had aroused the suspicions of some of their co-workers. Each of them was caught because of one death and subsequently confessed to many more. Each was able to obtain a plea bargain to avoid the death penalty in exchange for a full confession because only he knew the names of his other victims.

Both Donald Harvey and Charles Cullen left no trails for the police to follow, because their victims fit no pattern other than being patients in hospitals where the two worked, Cullen as a nurse and Harvey as a nursing assistant. Their motives for killing defied analysis. Even Harvey and Cullen can't explain why these particular victims were chosen and others spared. Both claimed that their motivation was to put suffering patients out of their misery.

Lax personnel policies appear to have been responsible for failures of the system with regard to screening these two killers from positions in which they could perform their lethal practices. Harvey had been allowed to resign from two hospitals under questionable circumstances. Cullen had been fired from at least two hospitals and allowed to resign from another during an inquiry. Both had histories of alcoholism, attempted suicide, and psychiatric care for depression. Strangely, both had apparently attempted suicide by setting fires in enclosed spaces with the expectation of being overcome by smoke.

On other dimensions, the differences between Donald Harvey and Charles Cullen are great. Harvey grew up in extreme poverty in rural Kentucky. Cullen's early life was in a working-class neighborhood in New Jersey. Harvey was the oldest of three children. Cullen was the youngest of nine. Harvey is openly homosexual, while Cullen was married (now divorced) and has two daughters. Harvey killed by a variety of methods, experimenting with different poisons. Cullen was far more technical, efficiently dispatching his victims with injections of overdoses of medicines or the wrong medicines.

The two had one horrifying behavior in common: from their positions as trusted providers of heath, they instead provided death to patients.

Donald recently said that he exchanged some correspondence several years ago with a young man in New Jersey who initiated the contact and said that he thought the two of them had a lot in common. He now thinks that correspondent may have been Charles Cullen. He did not tell Frassinelli about that.

29. Inmate #199449

As an attorney, I frequently visit clients in various places of incarceration, and thus I am familiar with the procedures for such visits and with the ambience of prisons. Such is not the case for someone who is unaccustomed to visiting prisoners. My co-author, Bruce Martin, describes below his experience in visiting Donald Harvey for the first time:

> Obviously, I needed to interview Donald, and I was eager to do so; but I was apprehensive—perhaps more about the place than about him. I felt I knew him because of the many hours I had watched him and listened to him on videotape. I had been inside prisons only twice before. Once was on a highly-structured group tour of a federal penitentiary many years ago, having no direct contact with any prisoners. The other was a prisoner-of-war camp our division guarded in Germany, where we treated our prisoners as equals who just happened to be on the losing side.
>
> My apprehension began with the preliminary arrangements, not so much because of the procedures as because of the necessity for making them. Bill Whalen actually took care of the paperwork. I needed Donald Harvey's formal permission for the interview, which he was quite willing to give. For me, this was no barrier, but Donald will not grant permission for any interview not approved by Bill. Then I needed permission from the prison authorities. Bill satisfied their requirements, and we were assigned a precise time and length for the interview. I was given a

sixteen-page document of rules for contacts with the media. I had never thought of myself as a member of the media, although of course I was, but the categorization jarred me.

Bill, paralegal Paula Ehemann, and I drove to Lebanon at the appointed time. Chatter in the car came to a halt as we came within sight of Warren Correctional Institution. The view of the prison is not grim and foreboding, so it was just the idea of the place. In fact, the prison blends in rather well with the semi-rural, light industrial area in which it is located. The approach is well landscaped. Only the coils of razor wire on the high fence and the ubiquitous towers with floodlights and surveillance cameras proclaim the nature of the institution.

The parking lot is, of course, outside the fence. We parked and walked a short distance to the gatehouse, which is considerably larger than that for a factory of comparable size. We entered a building that reminded me of a small regional air terminal. Once inside, we presented our credentials and identification. Bill was recognized and greeted, but was still subjected to the entrance routine. The contents of my briefcase were scrutinized, and I had to produce authorization for my tape recorder. Bill's papers were not subject to examination, because of his position as Donald's attorney, but mine were.

We emptied our pockets into the baskets provided and were directed through metal detectors like those at an airport. I was concerned, because I have an implanted pacemaker; but I was permitted to bypass the metal detector, having a tactile search and scanning with a hand-held detector instead.

Our left hands were stamped with a fluorescent ink like that used at nightclubs for exit and readmission.

Reunited with our possessions, we walked through a short hallway to a set of locked doors. A guard unlocked the doors, admitting us into a vestibule and locking the doors behind us. He then unlocked a second set of doors, which led to an open area behind the guardhouse. I felt a quiver of anxiety as I realized that we were securely locked in the prison, and the only way we could leave was for someone to let us out.

An escort met us as we passed through the doorway. Bill introduced me, and we talked for a few minutes about our purpose in making the visit. He then led us across a campus to another building. I was impressed with the well-tended lawn and flower beds surrounding it. Although I was reminded of college campuses, there were two striking differences. Nowhere did I see any foot-worn path that cut across between the paved walkways, and there was a complete absence of litter. Also, I saw no one else in the area except two men who appeared to be weeding the flower beds.

We entered a separate building smaller than a typical plant office, and our escort turned us over to a guide who led us to a cramped conference room, leaving us alone there briefly. He returned leading Donald Harvey and an armed guard. Bill and Paula greeted Donald, and Bill introduced him to me. We shook hands and took seats around the small conference table.

Donald's appearance was a surprise to me only in that he looked to be more mature than I had expected. I realized that considerable time had passed since most of the videotapes I had studied. I saw a neat, well-groomed man who could have passed for a corporate middle manager had he been wearing a suit and tie. Even in his prison clothes, he looked like a businessman. I had the impression that he was our host.

Presumably the guard was there to protect us, but I felt no need for protection and felt more like I was the one under surveillance. To the extent that I was aware of the guard, I was more concerned that I not violate any of the rules for visitors. She sat silently at the end of the table throughout the interview. Donald was obviously always aware of her presence, because once he glanced at her and then declined to answer one of my questions.

Donald was calm, polite, pleasant, soft-spoken, and cooperative. A few times he looked to Bill for a sign as to whether he should answer a particular question, but he was never evasive. He demonstrated his subtle sense of humor with little quips delivered with a smile. I could not reconcile the man I saw before me with the man who took the lives of so many people, and I didn't try.

At the end of the interview, our escort returned to lead us to the exit. First we submitted our left hands for scanning by ultraviolet light and our identification was verified. We were escorted to the double set of locked doors, where the process of sequential unlocking permitted us to pass through. After one more scanning of our stamped hands by black light, we were free to reenter the outside world.

* * *

Donald has adjusted to his circumstances. Responding to a question about prison life, he said, "My life is pretty much like yours, except for being locked down, being able to move around—I can't go any place. I work Monday through Friday. I get up and have three meals a day. I go to work. I work from seven to ten and noon to three, six hours a day. I'm off Saturdays, Sundays, and holidays. I watch TV in the evening, and I walk for exercise."

The exception is huge. He has not been outside the fence of Warren Correctional Institution at all since 1995, when he was taken to Columbus for an eye examination. He has mild cataracts, still not bad enough for an operation. Within the prison, he is confined to a limited area unless accompanied by an escort. Each night he is locked in his cell from 9:00 P.M. until 6:30 A.M.

Donald does not have the same degree of freedom as the general population of inmates, because he is in protective custody, or "PC." PC is not punitive; inmates are placed in PC for their own protection, not because they are considered a threat to others. Donald said he was told he was placed in PC because of an anonymous threat, or "kite," sent through the internal mail system when he was at the Lucasville penitentiary. He thinks it may have really been a pre-emptive decision because of the notoriety of his murder convictions. Somebody might have it in for him.

Meals are served in a chow hall. Mealtimes are earlier for inmates in PC than for the general population. Breakfast is 6:30–7:30, lunch 10:00–11:30, dinner 4:00–5:30. If needed, the same dining hall may be used for the general population after those in PC finish. Inmates eat with heavy plastic forks and spoons. They do not have table knives. Donald laughed when asked about that and said, "You could take anything and make a weapon out of it."

Inmates in PC have the same privileges as inmates in the general population to the extent that is feasible. For some time in the past, there were annoying exceptions because of logistical considerations (no television and no ice cream were the ones that bothered Donald the most). That was fixed ten years ago. Currently the only significant exception is that on the rare occasions when there is entertainment in the recreation hall, inmates in PC are excluded.

All inmates do have television available now, with a choice of several channels. One channel always carries a movie. Donald likes the movies, and they have first-run movies available, although he says the selections are sometimes really bad. He follows the news regularly on television and in *USA Today,* to which his sister subscribed for him.

The inmates in PC are not normally separated from each other. Although their section of the prison will accommodate seventy prisoners, it is not full. Donald has friends in PC, but there are some others he does not care to associate with.

Until recently, he had worked as a clerk in the Safety and Health Department. He told the name of his department with a slight smile, conscious that the assignment sounded incongruous for a serial killer. However, he had no direct contact with other inmates in his job. When he had any dealings with inmates in the general population, they met through a plate glass window as in a bank or through bars, ostensibly for his protection, not theirs. His duties included typing, filing, and making all kinds of badges used in the institution. He helped process new inmates.

Donald said his job was boring most of the time, but it was something to do. He worked thirty hours a week for twenty-four dollars a month, which paid for incidentals. He was paid in store credits.

He said that jobs in Ohio Penal Industries, which produces products such as furniture, are not available to inmates in PC, but that does not bother him. He didn't want to change jobs, even though some of the other jobs paid more, up to eighty dollars per month. He said he had one of the best jobs in the institution.

Donald was conscientious about his job and strived to do it well. In January 1990 he wrote me:

"This week I've been working several hours each day typing—on a good day I can type forty-five words a minute without a mistake. I had eighteen weeks of typing school in late '71 and early '72. I was taught on the old World War II Underwood, where you needed a hammer to move the keys, but my new computer-electric job is a dream. My typing speed is picking up, so I am on my way to becoming a whiz kid."

He sent me a copy of his evaluation report dated July 9, 2003. He was rated on seven aspects of his performance: attitude, initiative, quality/quantity, attendance, dependability, safety/housekeeping, and increasing knowledge/skills. On each of the seven aspects, he was rated ten on a scale of one to ten. His evaluator commented, "Very good worker. Very dependable. Always willing to help out."

He has recently changed jobs, because of a rule restricting the length of time an inmate may remain in the same job. He is currently working in the laundry, where he earns only eighteen dollars a month. He hopes the change is temporary and that he will be able to return to his position as a clerk as soon as he has met the administrative requirement. He said they want him back.

Each inmate has a visiting list consisting of family members and up to two friends. They can visit up to twice a month. Each visit is for a maximum of three hours, noon–3:00 P.M., or 4:30 P.M–7:30 P.M. For the convenience of those who live far from the prison, the two visits for a month can be on the same day or successive days. He can have special visitors by prior arrangement every ninety days. It takes about three weeks to arrange such a visit.

Visitors must pass through the security checkpoints entering and leaving. They meet with the inmates in a common room in a building close to the entrance, where they sit around small tables under the eyes of two guards seated at a slightly raised dais. The guards do not listen in on the conversations, although there is limited privacy because of the number of people gathered in the room. Soft drinks and snacks are available from a vending machine, but the visitor must be the one to get them. The inmate cannot act as "host."

Donald's sister, Pat, visits regularly, once or twice a month. Donald said they talk about family news, world news, movies they have seen, or anything else that might come up. His mother, who lives over 150 miles away, comes at about three-month intervals. Donald's brother, Tony, does not visit him. Donald said Tony denies their relationship.

Mail is not censored, but all incoming mail is examined for contraband, and letters may be read. Letters from me, his attorney, are examined for contraband, but are opened in front of Donald and not read.

Donald cannot receive telephone calls, but he can place collect calls, limited to fifteen minutes at a time.

He still cares about his appearance. The inmates have laundry washers, dryers, and irons available to them, and Donald keeps his cloths clean and well-pressed. He shaves regularly and keeps his mustache well-trimmed. In response to a question about razors, he says they are permitted. In fact, they are sold in the commissary. (That was not the case when he was held in the county jail. There prisoners could use razors only under supervision and had to return them to a guard.) Each unit has barber tools (no scissors), and inmates cut each other's hair.

Inmates are permitted exercise within their compound and in the gymnasium. Donald's choice is walking. He said he walks about thirty miles a week.

Although borderline diabetic, Donald is in generally good health. He has lost thirty-five pounds through his exercise program. He had gained about fifty pounds in prison, so he felt he needed to lose the weight and is pleased with himself. He considers himself lucky that he escaped AIDS, considering his promiscuous sex life when he was young and the practices of some of his partners. He claims to have had a slight stroke in 1987, but that is not a matter of record.

Donald continues to search for a religious foundation. After dabbling in Catholicism and Mormonism and practicing the occult, his latest exploration is Judaism. He said that a rabbi visits him regularly in the penitentiary.

He said that he still feels that what he was doing when he hastened the deaths of patients was right. He said that the few other deaths he caused were for self-preservation.

Asked what he misses most by being in prison, he answered promptly, "Freedom to get out and about."

He has adjusted to life in prison, accepting that the way it is now is the way it is going to be for him. He said that educational programs are not available to him, being limited to inmates who have a chance of release within five years. He has no ambitions or goals for change.

30. Reflections

People ask me, "Why did Donald Harvey kill all those people?"

I reply, "Because he could," which isn't a very satisfactory answer. But I think that really explains his actions.

All kinds of experts—police, prosecutors, psychologists and psychiatrists, criminologists, television commentators—try to fit Donald into some kind of classification system, but he falls outside their models. Whenever anyone says, "People like Donald Harvey. . . ," I know I am going to disagree with the rest of what is said. There are no other people like Donald Harvey. He is one of a kind.

Criminalists classify motives for murder in six to eight categories, depending on whose list you consider. In 1924, F. Tennyson Jones proposed a list of six categories:

Murder for gain
Murder for revenge
Murder for elimination
Murder for jealousy
Murder from conviction
Murder for the lust of killing

Additional categories have been suggested:
Murder for the thrill of the act
Murder for hate

While some of Donald Harvey's murders can be classified under this system, particularly some of the murders and attempted murders outside the hospitals where he worked, most of his murders defy being put into any of these categories.

Dr. Tanay tried to fit Harvey's murders into the category of "lust for killing," but his analysis does not fit the data. To support his thesis, Tanay cited the period when Harvey was working as a morgue attendant at the VA hospital, ignoring two key facts: (1) During that time, he had no access to patients, and (2) he continued to kill outside the hospital setting. Furthermore, when he was at Drake, Harvey helped perform autopsies on some of his victims, because he was a backup for the morgue.

Donald Harvey does not fit the generally accepted profile of a serial killer. He is a white male, which is characteristic, but otherwise he differs from the model described in most serious analyses.

According to Mauro V. Corvasce and Joseph R. Pagliano *(Murder One*, Writer's Digest Books, 1997), most serial killers are aged twenty-two to fifty. Harvey began when he was eighteen years old. Most serial killers employ one method of killing, with minor variations of that method to fit the circumstances. Harvey used suffocation, deprivation of life support such as turning off oxygen supply or using faulty equipment, poisoning, and shoving a coat-hanger through a catheter. He used a variety of poisons: arsenic, cyanide, morphine, rat poison, and adhesive cleaner. He administered poisons in food and drink, both orally and through feeding tubes, and by injection.

Studies describe serial murders as violent acts, typically with mutilation of the bodies. With rare exceptions, Harvey's killings were superficially peaceful acts. He was often absent when the victims died.

Most serial murderers choose victims of a particular type. Ted Bundy chose young, beautiful women with long hair. Harvey's victims were both male and female, Caucasian and African-American, with an age spread of over forty years. Although many were helpless patients in hospitals, a significant number of them were not.

Either intentionally or unintentionally, most serial killers leave their victims with what profilers call a "signature," distinctive features of the killings that link their crimes. Signatures may be sexual abuse of the victim, mutilation in specific ways, taking tokens, leaving notes or other characteristic items, positioning the bodies in bizarre poses, or disposing of bodies in particular locations. Harvey did none of these things. Although he said he took a few tokens, there was no pattern in what he took and he didn't preserve them.

In short, the "typical" serial killer leaves a trail of distinctive murders that eventually lead the police to the killer. Donald Harvey left no such trail. The only common feature was Donald Harvey himself. The killer led the police to the victims.

The model profile of a serial killer describes him as a loner. Donald made friends easily and had numerous relationships of long standing. He enjoyed being with people and joined organizations to further such activities. We know of only one indication of loner tendencies. Marie Eveleigh, who operated the gift shop at Drake (which now bears her name), told us that he would come into the shop every day to buy a snack at lunchtime and was always alone.

According to the behavioral scientists, sexual dysfunction is a typical characteristic of serial killers. Donald Harvey was sexually active. He was openly homosexual and had many sexual partners. Much of his adult life he lived with a lover. He was also capable of heterosexual intercourse. He claims to have fathered two sons.

The sexual abuse Donald experienced as a child undoubtedly had major effects upon his subsequent life. The relationship to his murders is not so clear. Donald himself has given three contradictory versions.

He has, on occasion, denied that there is any connection. There appear to be no sexual aspects to the deaths he caused. Any influence must be more subtle than that.

Donald has expressed the thought that when he killed his first victim, he was killing his abusers. Neither the circumstances nor the manner of death suggest that he was viewing the victim as a proxy for his abusers and was venting a delayed rage. He had a current anger directed specifically at the victim and acted spontaneously. His comment was probably metaphorical; he also said he was killing the Donald Harvey who had been abused as a child.

On other occasions, Donald implied that he identified with his victims. Donald had always been on the receiving end of interactions. He didn't do things to other people; they did things to him. Suddenly, he found that he was the one in control. In this interpretation, the sexual nature of his childhood abuse is less important than his helplessness. The operative word is probably control.

From the hospital staff's response to his first two instances of induced deaths—one spontaneous and one accidental—Donald learned the critical lesson: He could kill and get away with it.

In one other aspect of the theorists' model of a serial killer, Donald Harvey statistically fits the mold. Several studies have found that serial killers are likely to have suffered a significant head injury at some time before embarking on their criminal activities. Donald had such an injury as an infant and again in childhood. Causality has not been established. Certainly many people have had such injuries without becoming killers.

One theory is that somehow a part of the brain that serves as an inhibiting factor has been damaged. Donald Harvey has no guilt feelings. Intellectually, he knows that killing is wrong, but that knowledge has no emotional impact on him. He has regret for some of the consequences of his acts—for the families of his victims and for his own family—but he does not feel remorse. Donald can discuss murders he has committed with less emotion that someone else might show in discussing a poor investment.

The role of Donald's interest in the occult is uncertain. He has denied that there was a relationship between those beliefs and his murders, but he did regularly consult Duncan, his otherworld spiritual guide, about his plans. He seems to have believed in the existence of that guide. On one occasion, he said that Duncan was another aspect of himself and implied that he could be a reincarnation of Duncan. However, his killings preceded his initiation, and many were opportunistic, without reference to Duncan. He observed no occult rituals in his killings except the taking of tokens for later use.

After his conviction and sentencing and the subsequent publicity, Donald became interested in other serial killers and sought information about them. I tried to discourage that interest. I believe it led to the next strange episode in Donald Harvey's story and the second time he chose not to follow my advice.

In December 1988 Donald informed me that he had remembered seven more murders or attempted murders at Drake. I was doubtful of his claim and suspected he had some strange objective in mind, perhaps related to his liking publicity. It didn't seem reasonable to me that he could remember more after so much time had passed. He had felt very strongly the incentive to confess to everything under the plea bargain, and with the six additions in February the case had been closed. Ney had no interest in any further investigation, and the risk to Donald that another case might be uncovered was minimal. I advised him to drop it.

Donald gave me the seven names and described the killings. One of the persons he claimed to have killed was Ruth Gillispie. It was inconceivable to me that he had "just remembered" Ruth Gillispie. He had repeatedly denied in his confession and in responding to the civil suit that he had done anything to harm her. He had no incentive to deny any deaths when he was complying with the plea bargain and a very strong incentive for a complete confession. Why would he want to claim responsibility for her death at this late time?

For another of his newly claimed victims, he said that his motive was to have the opportunity to assist in her autopsy. He claimed that he was scheduled to work in the morgue, and he wanted to demonstrate to his superiors that he was competent to handle an autopsy for a patient who had been in isolation for infectious disease. While I couldn't deny that the motive was plausible for Donald, I couldn't believe his claim. How could he possibly have forgotten that victim when he was giving his detailed confession?

I concluded that Donald was attempting to claim responsibility for deaths he did not cause in order to "pad his statistics." I think he was feeling competitive with Ted Bundy, whose case was much in the news. I advised him against reopening his case. I reminded him that he had gone against my advice once before, when he talked to the FBI. He had been fortunate that the FBI decided against prosecution.

Donald insisted that he wanted to proceed. I reluctantly wrote a letter to Art Ney informing him that Harvey wished to confess to seven more victims.

Ney couldn't ignore the information. He took a delegation, consisting of Joe Deters, Terry Gaines, and himself to Warren County Correctional Institution to take a deposition from Harvey. As his attorney, I accompanied them.

Gaines read Donald his rights and then added, "You have violated the plea agreement by holding these names back. If we can prove one more case, we will seek the death penalty."

I thought we would have a strong case if I argued that the plea bargain would still protect Donald, but I decided against raising the issue at that time. I thought I saw through Ney's strategy and hoped it would work. None of us had any appetite for bringing the case to public attention again.

Donald's face registered shock. He looked to me for guidance, but I gave him no clue as to my thoughts. He already had my advice. He clammed up completely. Not one word.

When Ney recognized that Donald had chosen to exercise his right to remain silent, he indicated to the guard that the interrogation was over.

Donald never disregarded my advice again. He is the best client I ever had.

The prosecutors did get something out of the trip—a laugh at my expense. Not because of what I think Art Ney would agree was a successful fiasco, but because of an incident on the way home.

The four of us were in the county car, with Terry Gaines driving. Gaines had a heavy foot, and a highway patrolman pulled us over for speeding. Asked to produce his driver's license, Gaines also showed his badge as assistant prosecutor. The officer asked Art Ney for his ID, and he held out his badge for view. Joe Deters showed the officer his badge also. The officer looked in at me and asked Ney, "Are all of you guys prosecutors?"

"No. He's our prisoner."

The officer put away his book. He looked at me. "I don't know what you did, but you are in deep shit." He turned back to Gaines, "Well, hold it down the rest of the way. Okay?"

I let them have their laugh. I was happy that Donald's foolishness hadn't had worse consequences.

Donald wants his story told, although he knows he cannot profit financially. I sometimes suspect his motives, because he likes his notoriety. But I feel he is sincere when he says, "I want to do whatever I can to prevent anyone else from doing what I did. I wouldn't wish my life on my worst enemy."

As a measure of reparation, Donald presented his recommendations for steps to prevent health care personnel from killing patients. He would place much of the responsibility on the security employees. He said hospital security personnel should:

· not get too friendly with the nursing staff

· make their rounds on a random schedule

· wear quiet shoes

· not wear large rings of keys that rattle and announce their arrival

· have more shakedowns and pat hospital employees down

- stop hospital people and ask them to explain why they are in a particular area

- require people to answer questions

He said that the hospital administration should look for statistics that indicate abnormal death rates and also watch for overdoses.

Based on what I learned from Donald, I aided Communicorp.net in preparing an instructional videotape for the International Association for Health Care Security and Safety. My recommendations were for the nursing staff, essentially a reminder to be alert for things that were different from normal and might indicate a problem:

- a room door that was closed when it would normally be open

- a trash can placed so that it would create a noise if anyone entered a room.

- a drape closed around a bed for no apparent valid reason

- a medicine cart blocking a door

- items that could be used to cause death, such as a pillow out of place, a plastic garbage bag lying on a bed, a wet towel, adhesive cleaner, or a syringe

Human resources professionals also have something to learn from Donald Harvey's story. Jan Taylor's downfall came about because of flaws in the overall system regarding recommendations from former employers, and an improper response to the resulting difficulties.

America is the land of the lawsuit. In order to avoid litigation from former employees, many employers will say nothing negative when a prospective employer is checking references or employment history. Frustrated, employment specialists have become less diligent in checking information obtained from candidates for employment. They are thereby exposing themselves to charges of negligent hire.

Donald Harvey slipped through the system to obtain a position at Drake Memorial Hospital that he never should have held. When Jan Taylor learned that Donald Harvey was about to be arrested for murdering a patient, he falsified records to indicate a pre-employment reference check that didn't take place until long after Harvey was hired.

In Donald Harvey's case, our system of criminal justice passed a severe test. The situation was unprecedented, and we had to be creative. A serial killer was not released into the community to kill again. We found out who his victims were. Donald will be in prison for the rest of his life, with no chance of parole. The courts have been spared an endless round of appeals. Donald has been spared the uncertainty of existing on death row for years. He is secure in prison and able to be productive in a prison job.

The system works.

AFTERWORD

by Pat Minarcin

Let me say this squarely. The Donald Harvey I know is a serial killer, plain and simple.

He would have you believe that he was merciful. That he did what he did out of pity. That we should judge him sympathetically now, if we must judge him at all.

He is lying, from where I sit. And he is where he belongs—in prison for the rest of his life, passing his days in the company of ghosts.

For those of you who don't know of Harvey or the horrors he inflicted, he was once a hospital orderly. His last job was on Ward C-300 at a large county-owned convalescent hospital in Cincinnati.

When I knew it, Daniel Drake Memorial Hospital was a decent enough place—a little worn and dreary, perhaps, but a place of good intentions. Its mission was to provide long-term care for the sick who no longer required the more intense environment of a full-fledged hospital, but who still were too ill to go anywhere else.

Its patients included stroke and cancer victims, people with chronic heart disease and dementia, and still others seriously ill on some other account. Some could move around with little or no assistance. Some were on ventilators. A number would die at Drake. Others eventually would recover enough to be sent home or to a nursing home.

As with any hospital, Drake operated on a presumption of good faith. The people in white who worked there were assumed to be doing so because they wanted to help heal others. No one had reason to imagine that a killer might slip into this place.

Yet that is how the Donald Harveys of this world manage to thrive. As a rule, they are intelligent and wily. They learn early how to disguise themselves—with a smile, a small display of helplessness, perhaps wearing the uniform of someone we'd normally associate with kindness.

But behind this mask they seethe. And in a wink, once their prey is disarmed, they kill.

No matter that Harvey might have us think otherwise. Mercy doesn't enter into it.

And yet there is merit in listening to him, I believe, although I expect some to be appalled that Harvey is speaking to us at all.

Serial killers have turned up in places such as Drake before Harvey, and since. Indeed, not long after Harvey was unmasked, a male nurse was found to be killing patients in a hospital on Long Island. The nurse later said he had been motivated partly by what Harvey did.

It so happened that some of the medical authorities who helped catch that nurse had come to Cincinnati at my request a few months before to study the available records in the Harvey case. They went home with a heightened awareness, they later said, that helped them quickly solve the Long Island killings.

Perhaps hearing what Harvey says and how he says it will help someone else solve a similar crime, with the result that at least some lives may be saved.

I didn't know Bill Whalen when Donald Harvey stumbled into both our lives. I was the news anchor and managing editor at WCPO-TV, the fellow who with Carol Williams told Cincinnati every evening what was new in the world. Whalen, meanwhile, was a former prosecutor who had gone into private practice.

It was difficult for him at first, I believe. To make ends meet, he had signed up with the public defender's office to represent people accused of crimes and who couldn't pay for an attorney on their own. Bill earned less than the going rate for these cases, but at least the money helped him pay the rent.

Whalen was asked to serve as Donald Harvey's public defender. Harvey already was in jail. A patient named John Powell had died at Drake. Powell had been in a motorcycle accident, wasn't wearing a helmet, and sustained severe brain injuries. He was sent to Drake after a length of time at University Hospital in Cincinnati.

Ohio law requires autopsies for victims of fatal accidents. The deputy coroner who performed Powell's found cyanide in his system, a lot of it. Powell had been murdered. The question was why. And by whom?

Cincinnati homicide detectives eventually came to suspect Harvey, and before long he confessed. He'd done it, he said, because he felt sorry for Powell, and because Powell reminded him of his father.

Soon Harvey was charged. He made his first court appearance in April 1987 on Opening Day—which in Cincinnati is a celebration of the Reds, baseball, spring, and the renewal of life all rolled into one. The prosecutor told the judge that Harvey was suspected of committing "some kind of mercy killing" at Drake.

The story was on the news that evening. The reporter who covered it for WCPO said Harvey was thirty-six and had been working in hospitals for most of his adult life. As the facts unfolded, I remember wondering why someone whose job for years had been to help people get well would suddenly decide to kill one of them instead. The thought came and went like a shadow. Something felt out of place.

A few evenings later, a woman telephoned and said she was a nurse who had worked with Harvey at Drake and suspected that he'd killed others. She gave me the names of other possible victims. Her voice shook. She wouldn't give me her name, but she promised to telephone again in a day or two.

For the next three months, I dug into the story in every spare moment—working late into the night, starting again early the next morning, staying with it through every weekend. By the end of the third week, I'd spoken with a number of nurses and nurses' aides on the ward where Harvey worked. Many also said they feared Harvey had killed others (although a few dismissed the idea) and had tried to warn higher-ups. Their list of potential victims grew steadily. Before long, a number of Drake patients—the ones who could move around by themselves—were helping, too. Many provided documents. One even told me how I could gain entry to the hospital's computer system—an idea I refused. And a number of people related to the victims helped, too—providing medical records, autopsy reports, photographs, and other material.

Although I didn't realize it at the time, one of the most crucial items I learned about in this period was a record of when and where Harvey worked. He had his regular shift on C-300, of course. But sometimes he would be pulled from there to cover for an aide on another ward who was sick or on vacation, or to substitute for an orderly who worked in the hospital morgue. The record in question showed when this happened. It was called a "pull sheet" and was kept at the nurses' station on C-300. That was the only copy of it.

Finally everything I'd gathered made it obvious that the nurses and aides almost certainly were right. The number of patient deaths on C-300 was up sharply. And the ward's death rate was significantly higher than those of other, similar wards at Drake.

It was time to call Whalen. We'd been hearing that his client might have been responsible for other deaths at Drake, I said. Did he know anything about this? Could he rule it out? Could I interview Harvey?

Whalen seemed surprised but didn't say much. Days later, however, he called back. Sounding rattled, he said, "I still can't tell you anything, but keep digging."

"What does that mean?" I asked. "Are you saying that other deaths can't be ruled out? If no others are at issue, can't you at least say that, off the record?"

The line was silent for a moment. Then Whalen said, "That's all I can say."

Now it was my turned to be rattled. "Off the record, you're saying it's possible? Is that what you're saying?"

"I've said all I can," Whalen answered. "Keep digging."

Then he hung up.

"Good God," I thought. He's suggesting it may be true.

At the hospital, meanwhile, the situation turned ever more bizarre. Hospital officials began holding staff meetings to say that they'd heard people were talking to me. They wanted it stopped. The police had told them Powell was Harvey's only victim, they said. But even if Harvey had killed others, they added, they were old and sick and going to die anyway. Everyone needed to shut up. If anyone was caught talking, they'd be fired.

The threats backfired. More hospital employees called me. Many were nurses. One was a physician. Others held administrative positions. They passed along more records. Several began keeping notes. And every time an investigator arrived from the police department or the coroner's office, we were tipped immediately with a telephone call.

The employees gradually drew themselves into three camps. Some believed the hospital and maybe others were covering up something, and were determined to see the truth emerge. Some thought those in the first group were traitors and were determined to stop them. And some thought the situation was absurd and just wished it would go away.

In time, a couple of people in the coroner's office began talking to me privately. Then a few police officers did, too. We also began consulting with experts from other jurisdictions. And Whalen agreed to meet me for lunch.

He was guarded at first, and looked tired and drawn. But after a while, he relaxed a little and urged me again to keep digging.

"Are you saying he did it?" I asked.

"I didn't say that," Bill countered.

"We're off the record," I promised.

"Then, yes, he has admitted to me that he killed more than one."

"How do I prove it?" I asked.

"I don't know," Bill replied. "But don't quit."

Attorneys, of course, are obligated to give their clients the best representation they can and are bound under a principle called attorney-client privilege to keep their secrets. Yet Whalen was telling me that Harvey probably was a serial killer. I wondered why, but didn't want to chance putting him on the defensive. Whatever his motive, he seemed to be trying to do the right thing, and for the moment that was more important than anything else.

About this time, a homicide detective telephoned me at work. Drake's chief administrator was complaining about the questions we were asking, he said. Could he and I talk?

We met at midnight in an out-of-the-way restaurant on the edge of downtown. I had a late dinner. The detective sipped a Coke. He was fifty-ish, had a deeply lined face, salt-and-pepper hair, and a penetrating gaze that gave away little and missed even less.

"Why are we here?" I asked. "Is it against the law to ask questions?" No, of course not, the detective said. The administrator had told him he'd heard that I'd claimed to have spoken with Harvey, and Harvey had told me he'd killed others besides Powell. Was that true? the detective asked. If I knew something, he said, he hoped I would cooperate.

It wasn't true, I said. I'd asked his lawyer for an interview with Harvey, but the attorney had refused.

We circled one another in this fashion for another few minutes. The detective wore a police radio under his sports coat, and a wire ran from his collar to an earpiece. Occasionally he'd put a hand to his left ear to listen. Then we would resume. Finally we got to the heart of the matter.

Yes, the detective said, he and his partner had considered whether Harvey might have killed others. But the coroner told them nothing could be proven medically and there was no point pursuing it. The coroner was the expert in such matters, he said. The police had to defer.

"What if a number of Harvey's co-workers were convinced that others had been killed?" I asked. "What if they had names?"

The detective shrugged. "It would be a hell of a story if it's true and you can prove it," he said.

Had they put the possibility of more killings to Harvey? I wondered. He couldn't discuss that, the detective said; it might jeopardize the case. And what did the detective know of Whalen, Harvey's attorney? Hadn't Whalen once been a prosecutor? Yes, the detective said. Through the years they'd worked a number of cases together, cop and prosecutor. "He's one of the most honorable men I've ever known," the detective said. "They don't come any better."

Shortly afterward, the police chief, Lawrence Whalen (no relation to Bill)— with whom I had tangled previously—sent Drake's chief administrator a letter saying more or less that the case was closed. The administrator quoted from it in a fresh round of staff meetings and threatened again to fire anyone caught talking to me. And on orders from him, Drake's chief of security began a leak investigation.

The administrator, Jan Taylor, also asked a staff physician to review the medical records of each patient who had died on the ward where Harvey worked. The physician was not asked to determine whether any of the patients might have been killed. Rather, Taylor wanted the physician to compare each patient's records to his or her death certificate. Then the physician was to answer this question: Could the patient actually have died from the cause of death listed on the death certificate? Yes, the physician said, they could. It struck me as the kind of question someone worried about lawsuits would ask. Nevertheless, Taylor now began telling the staff that the hospital had conducted its own investigation, and nothing suspicious had been found. Those who said otherwise were being hysterical, Taylor said. The talk had to stop.

Taylor refused repeated requests for an interview, but eventually the president of the hospital's board agreed to speak with me. Had the board considered the possibility, I asked, that Harvey might have killed others? Of course, she said. But even if there were additional victims, they were old and sick and were going to die anyway. No one wanted the hospital to become known as a "death motel," she said. And anyway, the police had investigated and found no evidence, and so had Jan Taylor. She was confident Harvey hadn't killed anyone else.

In time I persuaded a number of the nurses to do on-camera interviews, on the condition that their voices and faces would be disguised. I also kept putting questions to the many others who were helping us, and Bill Whalen and I began meeting from time to time for lunch.

One of those meals was in the dining room of the Omni Netherland Plaza downtown. It was crowded and noisy with the din of voices and the clatter of silverware and china. But we thought this activity might shield us a little. Our previous meetings had drawn curious looks from other lawyers around town and even a judge or two.

After we ordered, Bill showed me a scrap of paper torn from a small notebook. On it was a list of names. Most, I knew by now, were patients who had died on the ward where Harvey worked. One, however, was a name less recognizable. I memorized it as Whalen continued.

"Donald says there were more," he said. "But these are the only names he can remember right now without looking at records."

"These are from Harvey?" I asked. "He says he killed everyone on this list?"

"Yes," Bill replied. "Everyone."

"Does he know you're giving this to me?"

"Yes, I've told him everything."

"Why are you doing this?" There. The question was out.

"Because Donald deserves the best defense I can give him, like anyone else accused of breaking the law," Bill began. He chose his words with care. "If you put it all together, it's possible that someone else will, too. I know the detectives working the Powell death. They're not stupid. Donald is a serial killer. Does he deserve to be executed for that? That's not my decision, and I can't allow myself to think about it. My job is to represent him."

Whalen's eyes clouded and he paused for perhaps ten seconds, gathering his thoughts.

"That doesn't necessarily mean that I should fight to get him off," Whalen said. "It would be risky, but I might actually be able to do it in the Powell death. Without Donald's confession, the prosecutor's office doesn't have much of a case. And I believe there might be grounds for getting the confession thrown out. If that were to happen, Donald could move somewhere, change his name, and go right back to doing what he was doing."

He continued, "But that could backfire. You already have your suspicions. I don't know what anyone else is telling you, but at some point you're going to have to report what you know. And that could bring down the mountain. If somebody puts everything together, the coroner is going to have to start digging up bodies. And that's when my client will get a death sentence."

So Whalen essentially was setting the table for Harvey to be found out.

"I have to," Whalen said. "I've seen it happen once before. It was a rape case. There was this one prosecutor I worked with. I didn't like him much. Nobody did. He was a veteran, you know? He'd been through the wars. He fought to win every case. He was as tough as they come.

"But in this rape case, it looked like the defendant had done it before. Several times. Nobody could prove it for sure. But the defense attorney didn't know that. So this prosecutor, he negotiated a plea agreement. The defendant had to agree to be locked up for a long time in a place where he'd get counseling.

"So I asked this prosecutor why he'd done that. Shouldn't this guy be doing hard time in prison?

"And he said, 'Sometimes what's most important is to get the guy off the street where he can't hurt anybody else. I might have won the one count against him. But that would have been his first conviction, and under the law, he could have been released on parole at some point. This way, I'm sure. He's going to be out of circulation for a long time.'

"I'm sort of in the same place."

"And Harvey knows?" I asked.

"Yes. And he agrees. Any way you look at it, this is the best way to go."

Back at the office, I checked the last name on the list Whalen showed me. It was of a patient who had died on another ward at Drake. I pulled his death certificate, then checked it against Harvey's pull sheet from the nurses' station on C-300. And there it was: Harvey had worked a shift on his ward the night the patient died. Neither Harvey nor Whalen could have known that I would have a way to match everything—the patient's name, the time of his death, the ward he died on, and Harvey's hours and whereabouts in the hospital that night. And too much matched for it to have been coincidence. Harvey was a serial killer, and here was the proof.

And so it was that I reported one night in June, three months after John Powell's death, that Harvey might well have killed others. The nurses appeared, their faces and voices disguised, and told what they knew. Then, experts from other jurisdictions filled the screen. Every one said that had this happened on their watch, they would have assumed Harvey had killed others. In circumstances such as these, they said, it was almost impossible for the killer to be caught the first time. And if they had as much evidence as we did, they would already have requested a court order to begin exhuming bodies. It took every minute of the six o'clock news to tell the story. Sports and weather were canceled. So were commercials.

The authorities were apoplectic. A special grand jury was seated to begin an investigation. The chief prosecutor, Art Ney, suggested publicly that I might become a target if I didn't cooperate. Then the next bomb fell. Whalen met with Ney and proposed a plea agreement. Now Ney was incredulous. Whalen pressed; Harvey would disclose everything in exchange for life in prison.

"How many murders are we talking about?" Ney asked.

"More than one," Whalen answered.

A day or two later, Whalen told me he was getting nervous. Ney was dragging his feet responding.

The next morning, an assistant prosecutor called to ask if he and Ney could meet with me privately. They wanted to discuss something related to the Harvey case, he said, but it wasn't anything we could talk about by phone.

We met in an office building downtown at the appointed hour. It was a holiday. The building was practically empty. Ney, usually talkative, came straight to the point. A lot of people had died at Drake while Harvey worked there. It would be impossible to exhume every one of them. He'd heard that I'd interviewed Harvey, and supposedly Harvey had told me about other victims. Was that true? No, I said.

Ney pressed ahead: If I knew of other victims, could I name them? Then, barely pausing, he said he could understand if someone had given me such a list in confidence. But wasn't there a way I could pass it to him without anyone knowing? Could I leave it under a rock somewhere or in a phone booth?

No, I said. The reporter who violates one confidence never shares another. It would be a blatant ethical violation. Ohio had a law acknowledging this obligation, I said, and guaranteeing that journalists could not be compelled under any circumstances to reveal confidential sources.

Ney tried another approach. Maybe I should think about whether I was obstructing justice, he said. The company I worked for might have good libel lawyers. But what good would that do me in jail? Everybody had a price. What was mine? How could we make a bargain?

We can't, I said. I stood and left.

They were looking for a way around Whalen's proposal for a full confession and plea. After insisting for months that they didn't know of anything to investigate, they now knew they'd been wrong. Ney, the coroner, the police chief, the hospital and maybe a county commissioner or two with aspirations of higher office all were vulnerable. But they could neutralize this threat if they could just find a way around Whalen.

Whalen, growing edgier, gave Ney a deadline: Either he accepted Whalen's proposal now, or Whalen would pull it off the table. Ney capitulated. Harvey would disclose everything. In exchange, he would get life.

Harvey had so much to confess that it took two days—and even then he couldn't remember every victim's name. There were just too many. It was all recorded on videotape. Ney watched it over a feed piped into his office, along with the coroner, Frank Cleveland.

The special grand jury was seated shortly afterward. Many who worked at Drake were subpoenaed to testify. They waited nervously to be called into the grand jury room—nurses, aides, clerks, administrators. Many fled swiftly when they were excused, as if running from the horror they all shared. Some later said angrily that they were asked whether they had spoken with me. "We were trying to do the right thing," a nurse said later. "Nobody else was. What business did they have asking that?" More than one spoke of feeling violated.

The grand jurors also watched the video of Harvey's confession. Afterward, they were drained, some of them said. There was so much death, so much misery.

When Ney said he had nothing else for them, the grand jurors asked if they could write a report. So many failures had occurred, they said. The community had a right to know. Ney told them they couldn't. It was beyond the scope of the law, he said. A number of experts later challenged this sharply.

Finally came the day when Harvey's plea agreement had to be formalized in court. It was late summer and already hot out. The survivors of many of the victims crowded the courtroom, looking ashen and fanning themselves. Several held hands. Harvey and Whalen sat alone at the defense table.

Ney stood before the court exuding outrage and pointed at a signboard sitting on an easel. It listed Harvey's victims and the manner in which each died. Ney read them all and waxed indignant over the impression some might have that officials dropped the ball in the case. These people were some of the country's finest, he said.

At one point, Harvey leaned over and whispered something in Whalen's ear, and both laughed. A number of people touched by the case later voiced outrage over that moment. Whalen said Harvey was trying to compensate for being nervous. But some rejected this explanation and later accused Whalen of being almost as insensitive as the client he was representing.

Then Harvey pleaded guilty and the judge sentenced him to three terms of life in prison, plus a little extra for a few people he unsuccessfully tried to kill.

There were postscripts afterward—Harvey pleading guilty to more killings in Kentucky, a flurry of lawsuits, the sacking of Jan Taylor at Drake, the sudden retirement of the head nurse who had refused to listen to her staff's worries about Harvey and who threatened instead to fire them. But vital questions went unanswered. Why did all those warnings go unheeded?

And why had so many highly placed officials seemed so indifferent to the possibility that Harvey had killed others?

Ney told reporters afterward—as the coroner and police chief looked on impassively—that the investigation of Harvey hadn't ever stopped and would have led to the truth eventually. What we had done might have helped focus it, he said, but nothing else.

Based on everything I know, that was an exaggeration, to put it kindly.

At Drake, Taylor had done everything in his power to keep the truth from coming out, including threatening Drake employees with their jobs for exercising their First Amendment rights. The coroner, Frank Cleveland, had said there was no point investigating—no point to doing the work that every expert we consulted said they'd be doing if confronted with the same evidence. The police chief, Lawrence Whalen, had virtually declared the case closed. Taylor repeatedly threatened to hunt down and fire anyone at Drake caught talking (Taylor bitterly told me a year later that he was following orders and was betrayed, but he refused to say more). The president of Drake's board said she and her fellow directors didn't want the hospital to become known as a "death motel." The prosecutor, Art Ney, made it his mission to defend everyone else. And the county commissioners, who ultimately were responsible for Drake, avoided commenting on what had happened at the hospital until the very end. Was there a cover-up? Or were the people in charge just asleep at the switch? The available evidence suggests it was both.

This much is certain: The story wouldn't have come to light without a small army of heroes. The nurses and nurse's aides stand first in this line, in my opinion. They did the right thing in the face of terrible pressure. They weren't sophisticated about the law. For all they knew, they really could have been fired for what they did. Some were single parents who, had the worst happened, might have lost homes, savings, careers. And yet they didn't flinch.

The patients who stood with them also had much to lose. Had their role come to light, I imagine they'd have been put out of the hospital. In such a case, they might have lacked the legal protection the nurses and aides had. What's more, their ailments had rendered the majority of them jobless. Had they been put out, they wouldn't have had the resources to cope for very long. They knew this. And they did all they could anyway.

And then came the help from those who were the survivors of some of Harvey's victims. It must have been especially difficult for them. Some wept. But not once did they flinch.

I wish I could name all these people. They deserve to be recognized. But I don't have their permission.

It's the same with those who tried to help from within the system. Faced with having to choose between what their bosses were saying and doing, and their sense of justice, they chose the latter. They ran risks, too.

And finally, there is Bill Whalen. He was vilified after the enormity of Harvey's crimes was brought to light. Some speculated that he must have had a role in the story, thus insinuating that he must be guilty of something almost as awful as Harvey. I cannot imagine how these things sat with Whalen. But as far as I know, he never doubted the propriety or logic of what he did. Instead, he stayed his course, doing things very few knew about.

In murders, almost never is the person slain the killer's only victim. The dead person's survivors are victims, too. They grieve, as anyone else would after the death of someone close. But they also carry with them images of how their loved one must have died and punish themselves with a welter of what-ifs and what-might-have-beens for the rest of their lives. The survivors of Harvey's victims were no different.

To help, the county put together a victims' assistance program for them. And for a long time, many who lost loved ones to Harvey came together once a month through this effort to try to gain some degree of understanding.

I spoke to this group one evening. The sorrow and anger in the room was palpable. Several asked questions I couldn't answer—about Harvey, about the authorities, about Drake. I can't be sure, but I imagine that at least some of those questions haunt them to this day.

Bill Whalen met with this group, too. Whalen was under no obligation to do this, and as far as I know his doing so was never reported. He did it because he felt he should. It was simply the right thing to do, he said. The dead and the living both deserved it.

In a way, the same principle is in play here.

As I said at the beginning, Harvey lies in these pages, I believe. Brazenly, time and time again. Some will find what he says outrageous. Others will turn away and move quickly on. Still, twisted and lacking in credibility though it may be, this is his explanation.

And here is Whalen again, quietly helping to shed light on the tragedy.

It is not a role he would have chosen for himself, I believe, had he known what awaited him so long ago. But finding himself stuck in it, he did not turn away. He did as the nurses and aides did, and the patients, and those who survived the victims, and all the others who may always be anonymous as well.

The pity is that so many officials did not. They turned away and moved on—not wanting to know the truth, even though they suspected it—until they were forced to do otherwise.

The further pity is that they were the gatekeepers—of the hospital, of the law, of the city, and of the county. They were supposed to do better. And they did not.

—January 2005

EPILOGUE

by Bruce Martin

Who is Donald Harvey?

Is he a cold-bloodied serial killer, full of anger, who expressed his fury by killing helpless patients?

Is he a victim of poverty and child abuse whose adult behavior is a conditioned response to his childhood experiences?

Is he a compassionate person who took personal risks to free hopeless patients from a burden of life he would consider intolerable for himself?

Is he a typical example who fits the profiles psychiatrists and psychologists have cited to fit their particular theories about psychopathology?

Is he a self-delusional person who believes his own fantastic explanations for his anti-social behavior?

Is he two people, as he has sometimes claimed?

I don't know.

I have spent hours listening to and watching tapes of his interactions with diverse people in a wide variety of circumstances. I have read and listened to expositions by others regarding their opinions of Donald Harvey. I have read accounts he has written and his written comments on a draft of this book.

I have interviewed him and found him making a sincere effort to provide accurate information for this book. I have also interviewed him and found him playing games with me, deliberately trying to embarrass me, and delighting in confusing me with conflicting stories of the same events.

Readers will have to draw their own conclusions. Perhaps his own answer is the best: "I'm Donald Harvey." He's one of a kind. Thank God for that.

APPENDIX: VICTIMS

NAME	LOCATION	ACTION	DEATH	CONFESSION	INDICTED	CONVICTION	CHARGE
Alexander, Diane	Carl's home	1983	—	07/09/87	yes	08/18/87	attempted murder
Barney, Donald	Drake	07/07/86	07/07/86	07/09/87	yes	08/18/87	murder
Berndsen, Lawrence	Drake	04/20/86	—	01/21/88	yes	02/19/88	attempted murder
Bowling, William	Marymount	08/30/70	08/30/70	10/21/87	yes	11/02/87	murder
Buehlmann, Albert	Drake	10/29/86	10/29/86	07/09/87	yes	08/18/87	murder
Butner, Silas	Marymount	01/23/71	01/23/71	10/21/87	yes	11/02/87	murder
Canter, Milton	Drake	08/29/86	08/29/86	07/09/87	yes	08/18/87	murder
Carrroll, Sam	Marymount	01/09/71	01/09/71	10/21/87	no	—	—
Cody, Henry	Drake	11/86	11/04/86	07/09/87	yes	02/19/88	murder
Collins, William	Drake	10/30/86	10/30/86	07/09/87	yes	08/18/87	murder
Combs, John V.	Marymount	01/26/71	01/26/71	09/09/87	yes	11/02/87	murder
Crockett, Robert	Drake	06/29/86	06/29/86	07/09/87	yes	08/18/87	murder
Day, Odas	Drake	12/09/86	12/10/86	07/09/87	yes	08/18/87	murder
Evans, Logan D.	Marymount	05/30/70	05/30/70	10/21/87	no	—	—
Evans, Roger	Drake	09/17/86	09/17/86	07/09/87	yes	08/18/87	murder
Fish, Cleo	Drake	12/10/86	12/10/86	07/09/87	yes	08/18/87	murder
Frey, Earnest	Drake	08/86	08/16/86	07/09/87	yes	08/18/87	murder
Gilbert, Ben H.	Marymount	07/24/70	07/28/70	09/09/87	yes	11/02/87	murder
Harris, Joseph C.	VA hospital	—	—	07/16/87	no	—	—
Harrison, Margaret E.	Marymount	12/07/70	12/07/70	10/21/87	no	—	—
Hill, Doug	his home	1982	—	no	no	—	—
Hoeweler, Carl	his home	1982	—	07/09/87	yes	08/18/87	attempted murder
Hoeweler, Henry	Providence Hospital	04/25/83	05/01/83	07/09/87	yes	08/18/87	murder
Hoeweler, Margaret	Carl's home	—	—	07/09/87	no	—	—
Hood, Anna	Drake	07/20/86	08/86	01/21/88	yes	02/19/88	attempted murder
Johnson, Willie	Drake	05-06/86	—	01/21/88	yes	02/19/88	attempted murder
Kendrick, Clayborn	Drake	09/20/86	09/20/86	07/09/87	yes	08/18/87	murder
Kukro, Margaret	Drake	02/14/87	02/15/87	07/09/87	yes	08/18/87	murder
Leitz, Hilda	Drake	03/07/87	03/07/87	07/09/87	yes	08/18/87	murder
Lemon, Stella	Drake	02/87	03/16/87	07/09/87	yes	08/18/87	murder
McQueen, Eugene	Marymount	07/10/70	07/10/70	09/09/87	yes	11/02/87	voluntary manslaughter

NAME	LOCATION	ACTION	DEATH	CONFESSION	INDICTED	CONVICTION	CHARGE
Metzger, Helen	her home	04/83	04/10/83	07/09/87	yes	08/18/87	murder
Moore, Sterling	VA hospital	—	—	07/16/87	no	—	—
Nally, Doris	Drake	05/02/86	05/02/86	01/21/88	yes	02/19/88	murder
Nelson, Leon	Drake	04/12/86	04/12/86	07/09/87	yes	08/18/87	murder
Nichols, Maude	Marymount	08/15/70	08/15/70	10/21/87	yes	11/02/87	murder
Oldendick, John	Drake	—	08/01/86	07/09/87	yes	08/18/87	attempted murder
Parker, Leo	Drake	01/10/87	01/10/87	07/09/87	yes	08/18/87	murder
Peluso, James	Carl's home	11/84	11/09/84	07/09/87	yes	08/18/87	murder
Pike, Joseph	Drake	03/06/87	03/06/87	07/09/87	yes	08/18/87	murder
Powell, John	Drake	03/07/87	03/07/87	04/06/87	yes	08/18/87	murder
Proffit, Hiram	VA hospital	09/19/84	11/19/84	07/09/87	no	—	—
Rawlins, Maggie	Marymount	01/15/71	01/15/71	10/21/87	yes	11/02/87	murder
Rhodes, Harry	VA hospital	—	—	07/16/87	no	—	—
Ritter, James R.	VA hospital	—	—	07/16/87	no	—	—
Sasser, Milton Bryant	Marymount	03/14/71	03/14/71	10/21/87	no	—	—
Schreibeis, Edward	Drake	06/86	06/20/86	07/09/87	yes	08/18/87	murder
Thompson, Mose	Drake	11/22/86	11/22/86	07/09/87	yes	07/09/87	murder
Twitty, James A.	VA hospital	—	—	07/16/87	no	—	—
Tyree, James Harvey	Marymount	05/31/70	05/31/70	10/21/87	no	—	—
Vetter, Harold	Carl's home	—	—	no	no	—	—
Watson, Nathaniel	Drake	04/7-8/86	04/08/86	07/09/87	yes	02/19/88	murder
Weddle, Virgil	Drake	04/19/86	04/19/86	07/09/87	yes	08/18/87	murder
White, Harold	Drake	07/86	10/11/86	07/09/87	yes	08/18/87	attempted murder
Williams, Harve	Marymount	07/12/70	07/12/70	09/09/87	no	—	—
Wilson, Edward	his home	03/18/85	03/23/85	07/09/87	yes	08/18/87	murder
Woods, James	Drake	07/86	07/25/86	07/09/87	yes	08/18/87	murder
Wyan, Viola Reed	Marymount	11/04/70	11/04/70	09/09/87	yes	11/02/87	murder
Wyatt, Elizabeth	Marymount	06/22/70	06/22/70	09/09/87	yes	11/02/87	murder

INDEX

Cody, Henry, 100, 122–124, 133, 151
Cody, Lillie, 100
Collins, William, 99–100, 123, 132
Combs, John V., 72, 73, 159
Combs, Pat, 34, 59, 149–150, 173, 178, 186
Connelly, Terry, 50
Corvasce, Mauro V. (*Murder One*), 189
Crawford, Sandy, 177
Criminal Mind, The (Ramsland), 58
Crockett, Robert, 95, 122, 132
Crowe, Claude, 112
Crush, Judge, 41–42
Cullen, Charles, 179–180
cyanide
   carried by Harvey, 94, 101
   as cause of death, 19–22, 47, 94–104, 189
   detection of, after embalming, 37, 131
   distinctive odor of, 24, 25, 123
   dumped into Great Miami River, 29
   in Powell case, 19–22, 30
   properties of, 124, 130–131
   test for, 26

- D -

Daniel Drake Memorial Hospital, 18, 24, 28, 161, 194, 197, 202
   employee informants at, 38–40, 199, 200, 207
   media coverage of, 31, 37–38, 199
   Medicare and Medicaid decertification, 167–168
   scrutiny of hiring practices at, 166

Skilled Nursing Facility, 19, 89
   ward C–300, incidents of death in, 50–51, 204
Davis, Eric, 31
Day, Odas, 101–102, 123, 133
defense strategies
   alibi, 34
   mercy–killing, 34, 35, 41, 109, 126, 134, 138, 141, 197
   Not Guilty by Reason of Insanity (NGRI), 31, 34, 35, 44, 136
   plea bargain, 35, 109–118, 122, 125, 126, 129, 137, 142, 148– 151, 155–156, 158, 161–162, 170, 172, 179, 191, 192
   self-defense, 34
Detachol. *See* adhesive cleaner, as cause of death.
Deters, Joe, 112–115, 121–122, 130, 131, 133, 136, 146, 150, 151, 172, 192, 193
DiAngelo, Rich, 149
Dinkelacker, Pat, 112
Drake Hospital. *See* Daniel Drake Memorial Hospital.
Dresher, Hank, 120, 123
Duke, David, 81
Dumbar, Bruce, 178
Duncan (Harvey's spirit guide), 18, 20, 22, 78, 94, 100, 104–105, 174, 191

- E -

Ehemann, Paula, 182–183
Estes, Ken, 77
Evans, Logan D., 63–64

ABOUT THE AUTHORS

WILLIAM WHALEN was the court-appointed public defender for Donald Harvey.

He is a graduate of Villa Madonna College and Salmon P. Chase College of Law. After being admitted to the Ohio Bar Association, he entered private practice with Smith and Whalen in Mason, Ohio. He also has been admitted to the Kentucky Bar Association.

He was with the Hamilton County (Ohio) Prosecutor's office for fourteen years, two as assistant prosecuting attorney and twelve as assistant prosecutor.

Since returning to private practice in 1984, he has specialized in criminal defense. His other most significant cases have included:
- State of Ohio v. Deborah Brown. Brown, a serial killer, was convicted of eight killings.
- State of Ohio v. Lockland Police Department. Police Chief Ken Johnson was acquitted of all charges.

He is an adjunct professor at Mount St. Joseph College and lectures at Salmon P. Chase College of Law, Northern Kentucky University, and Miami University.

He is a reader for Radio Reading Services for the Blind and a server at the Fairhaven Rescue Mission for Men. He has served on the Board of Directors for Women Helping Women and as a member of the Rape Task Force.

He lives in Fort Wright, Kentucky.

BRUCE MARTIN began his professional career as a chemical engineer with the Procter & Gamble Company, after receiving a B.S. from Auburn University and an M.S. and Ph.D. from Ohio State. During thirty-two years with Procter & Gamble, he held a variety of technical and managerial positions in research and development and market research. He later joined Indumar Inc., where he served as Senior Vice President.

A dedicated teacher, he has been on the faculty at three universities: Auburn, Ohio State, and the University of Cincinnati. He currently moderates a course entitled "I Love a Mystery" for the Institute for Learning in Retirement at the University of Cincinnati.

He has received many honors during his career: Distinguished Alumnus, College of Engineering, Ohio State University; Distinguished Engineer, Technical Societies Council of Cincinnati; Chemical Engineer of the Year,

Ohio Valley Section, American Institute of Chemical Engineers (AIChE); and AIChE Marketing Hall of Fame.

He is the author of *Martin's Mini Mysteries* and co-author of *Killing Is Murder*, by Pleiades. Bruce is married to author Phyllis Martin. They live in Cincinnati, Ohio.

PAT MINARCIN was the news anchor and managing editor at station WCPO-TV in Cincinnati from September 1984 to September 1989. WCPO-TV was awarded a Peabody for exceptional service to the public for "Drake Hospital Investigation."